Songs Between the Storms:
Selahs for the Soul
Book One

Dave Joseph Jr.

*"I will sing of your strength,
in the morning I will sing of your love;
for you are my fortress,
my refuge in times of trouble."
—Psalm 59:16 (NIV)*

© 2025 Dave Joseph Jr.
All rights reserved.
No part of this book may be reproduced, stored in a retrieval system, or transmitted in any form or by any means—electronic, mechanical, photocopying, recording, or otherwise—without prior written permission from the publisher/author, except for brief quotations used in reviews or scholarly works.

Scripture quotations are taken from the Holy Bible,
New International Version® (NIV®),
New King James Version® (NKJV®), and
English Standard Version® (ESV®).
Used by permission. All rights reserved worldwide.
Scripture versions are noted where applicable.

ISBN: 978-1-944634-11-7
Contact the author:
www.poetpastor.substack.com

Dedication

For the ones who didn't wait for the storm to pass—
but stood in it, soaked in truth, and still chose to believe.

For the ones who whispered prayers in borrowed tongues,
who sang freedom songs in rooms where no one clapped,
who held the line when others broke rank—
not for applause,
but because they remembered who they were.

For the sons and daughters of **struggle and spirit**,
who carry their grandmother's Bible in one hand
and a broken world in the other.

For the gentle fathers, the fierce aunties,
the weary caregivers, the justice seekers,
and the midnight soul holders
who know that faith is more than feelings—
it's a fight.

And for every child still becoming,
every elder still teaching,
every soul still standing in the storm—
this book is your mirror.
Your melody.
Your reminder:

You are not forgotten.
You are not finished.
You are not alone.

—DCJ

Acknowledgments

To my family—
in the **Carolinas**, where our roots ran deep and our prayers ran deeper.
In the **Caribbean**, where songs rose from struggle and joy danced with the wind.
In the **Church**, where I first learned what it meant to tremble before truth
and be healed by holy hands that looked like mine.

To my **teachers**—
the English teachers who gave me words,
the Math teachers who taught me order in chaos,
and the Spanish teachers who reminded me
that God speaks every language,
and silence is often His best translation.

To those who purchase this book,
who share it with trembling hands and tear-washed eyes—
thank you.
You are sowing songs into the soil of someone else's storm.

To every **prayer lifted** over these pages,
even the quiet ones,
even the ones you never finished—
I felt them.
And God surely answered.
May this book bless you back
a hundredfold.

With grace,

Dave Joseph Jr.

How to Use This Book

An Invitation to Breathe Between the Lines
This is not a book to be rushed.
It is not a devotional to check off.
It is not poetry to impress or escape.

This book is a journey through silence—
the kind that follows weeping,
or waiting,
or wondering whether God still hears you.

Each poem in these pages is a **selah**—
a pause in the storm.
A breath between breakdown and breakthrough.
A sacred moment to reflect, release, and remember.

What You'll Find:

- **A Poem** — honest, raw, and poetic, shaped by the storm and pointing toward stillness.
- **Selah Reflection** — a short meditation to sit with the poem and let it settle into your soul.
- **Spiritual Challenge** — a small, courageous action to help you live what you've read, even if it's just one whispered prayer.

How to Read:

- Go **slow.** One poem at a time is enough.
- Let a phrase stop you.
- Linger in the lines that make your heart ache or heal.
- Write in the margins.
- Cry if you need to.
- Read aloud when your voice returns.

Some readers move through this over 77 days.
Others open to the page they need and let the words find them.
There is no wrong way—only the way that meets you honestly.

If You Journal:

You'll find space beside each poem or section to write what rises up.
Whether that's a prayer, a question, or a name you need to forgive—
put it on the page. God can handle your truth.

If You're in the Middle of Something:
This book was made for you.
Not the polished you.
Not the Sunday-best version.
But the quiet you.
The tired you.
The one still standing in the storm.

You don't need to be healed to begin.
You just need to show up to the page.

Take your time.
Let these pages be a rhythm,
a refuge,
and a reminder:

Even now—God is still speaking.
Even here—your soul can still sing.

Selah.

A Word Before the Wind Settles

There is a place between thunder and testimony.
A hush between the breakdown and the breakthrough.
A silence not of absence,
but of holy waiting.
It is here—in this sacred stillness—
we learn to listen

This book was not written in the sunshine.
It was carved in the quiet,
etched in the shadows,
stitched together with the trembling hands of someone
who kept breathing
even when the air felt thin.

What you hold is not just poetry.
It is survival.
It is spiritual resistance.
It is soul music sung softly
beneath the weight of the storm.

Selah
It's an ancient word.
It doesn't translate cleanly.
But oh, it speaks loudly.
Some say it means "pause."
Others, "lift up."
Still others, "stop and listen."

But I say this—
Selah is what we do
when our souls can't rush anymore.
When the questions get louder than the answers,
and God doesn't explain—
but He stays.

This is not a book to race through.
There are no fast answers here.
Only quiet truths that refuse to be rushed.
You may find yourself weeping mid-page.
Or exhaling after a line that breaks you open.
Let that be worship.

You will walk through wounds,
through waiting,
through weeping,
and finally—through wonder.

And if you've ever felt like you were the only one
still stuck in the middle,
this book is a gentle hand on your shoulder,
saying:
"You're not alone. Keep singing. Even softly."

So exhale.
Turn the page slowly.
Mark it up.
Cry when you need to.
Sing when you can.
And let the silence
do what only silence can:

Heal you. Hold you. Remake you.

Selah.

Dave Joseph Jr.

Songs Between the Storms: Selahs for the Soul

Wounds & Whispers

The ache before the voice.

When Tears Burn Quiet   19
  Psalm 56:8 – "Put my tears in Your bottle..."

Lament with No Return Address   21
  Psalm 139:1,4 – "Even before a word is on my tongue..."

Cracked Clay, Still Held   23
  2 Corinthians 4:7 – "We have this treasure in jars of clay..."

When the Mirror Lies   25
  1 Corinthians 13:12 – "Now we see in a mirror, dimly..."

The Ache Between Amens   27
  Romans 12:12 – "Be constant in prayer..."

God Doesn't Flinch   29
  Psalm 27:10 – "The Lord will hold me close."

The Cry Behind My Eyes   31
  Psalm 34:18 – "The Lord is near to the brokenhearted..."

I Named It Nothing   33
  Isaiah 61:3 – "Beauty for ashes..."

Hands Too Tired to Lift   35
  Exodus 17:12 – "They held up his hands..."

The Silence After the Shout   37
  Isaiah 30:15 – "In quietness and trust is your strength..."

I Still Belong   39
  Romans 8:16 – "We are children of God..."

Songs Between the Storms: Selahs for the Soul

Waiting in the Wind
Hope when nothing moves.

Held by a Thread   43
  Ecclesiastes 3:11 – "He has made everything beautiful in its time..."

The Clock That Doesn't Move   45
  Psalm 90:4 – "A thousand years in your sight are like a day that has just gone by..."

Still Doesn't Mean Stuck   47
  Exodus 14:14 – "The Lord will fight for you; you need only to be still."

When the Promise Feels Like a Lie   49
  Habakkuk 2:3 – "Though it linger, wait for it..."

Windless Worship   51
  John 4:23 – "True worshipers will worship the Father in spirit and truth..."

Nothing is Happening (And That's Something)   53
  Isaiah 40:31 – "But they that wait upon the Lord shall renew their strength..."

I Prayed, Then Waited, Then Doubted   55
  Mark 9:24 – "Lord, I believe; help my unbelief!"

The Weight of Waiting   57
  Psalm 27:14 – "Wait for the Lord; be strong..."

Tired of Hoping   59
  Proverbs 13:12 – "Hope deferred makes the heart sick..."

Stillness Is a Song   61
  Zephaniah 3:17 – "He will quiet you with His love..."

If the Wind Never Comes   63
  Daniel 3:18 – "But even if He does not..."

Bitter Waters & Better Promises

Holding on when healing delays.

Bitterness in My Mouth   67
    Exodus 15:23-25 – "When they came to Marah, they could not drink its water because it was bitter... and the Lord showed him a tree..."

This Wasn't the Plan   69
    Proverbs 16:9 – "The heart of man plans his way, but the Lord establishes his steps."

The Prayer I Prayed in Pieces   71
    Romans 8:26 – "...the Spirit Himself intercedes for us with groanings too deep for words."

I Forgave, but I Still Remember   73
    Ephesians 4:32 – "Be kind to one another... forgiving one another, as God in Christ forgave you."

Why Did You Let It Hurt?   75
    John 11:21 – "Lord, if You had been here, my brother would not have died."

I Want to Believe Again   77
    Mark 5:36 – "Do not fear, only believe."

The Promise Has Teeth   79
    2 Corinthians 1:20 – "For all the promises of God in Him are Yes and in Him Amen..."

Don't Let Bitterness Preach   81
    Hebrews 12:15 – "See to it that no bitter root grows up..."

He Met Me at Marah   83
    Psalm 34:8 – "Oh, taste and see that the Lord is good..."

It Was Sweet All Along   85
    Genesis 50:20 – "You intended to harm me, but God intended it for good..."

Better Than I Asked For   87
    Ephesians 3:20 – "Now to Him who is able to do exceedingly abundantly above all..."

Songs Between the Storms: Selahs for the Soul

Midnight Melodies

Worship in the dark.

When the Song is a Whisper — 91
  Psalm 42:8 – "At night his song is with me…"

The Chains Didn't Break First — 93
  Acts 16:25–26 – "Paul and Silas were praying and singing hymns… and suddenly there was a great earthquake…"

I Sing So I Don't Surrender — 95
  Psalm 59:16 – "I will sing of your strength… for you have been my fortress…"

Silence is Still a Sound — 97
  Psalm 62:1 – "For God alone my soul waits in silence…"

Midnight Feels Like Forever — 99
  Lamentations 3:23 – "Great is Your faithfulness… your mercies are new every morning."

My Song is Off-Key, But It's Mine — 101
  Psalm 100:1 – "Make a joyful noise unto the Lord…"

The Night I Prayed Without Words — 103
  Romans 8:26 – "The Spirit Himself intercedes…"

There's a Hallelujah in the Hurt — 105
  Psalm 34:1 – "I will bless the Lord at all times…"

Before the Earthquake, There Was Worship — 107
  Acts 16:25 – "About midnight Paul and Silas were praying and singing hymns to God…"

Dark Doesn't Mean Defeated — 109
  John 1:5 – "The light shines in the darkness, and the darkness has not overcome it."

This Night Will Not Last Forever — 111
  Psalm 30:5 – "Weeping may endure for a night, but joy comes in the morning."

Songs Between the Storms: Selahs for the Soul

The Weight of Grace

When mercy feels too heavy to carry.

When Grace Feels Too Heavy to Hold   115
    Romans 5:20 – "Where sin abounded, grace abounded much more."

This Mercy Makes Me Tremble   117
    Hebrews 4:16 – "Come boldly to the throne of grace..."

I Don't Deserve This (And That's the Point)   119
    Ephesians 2:8 – "By grace you have been saved..."

Forgiven Doesn't Mean Forgotten   121
    Isaiah 43:25 – "I... remember your sins no more."

The Shame Grace Refused to Carry   123
    Romans 8:1 – "There is now no condemnation..."

The Grace I Can't Repay   125
    Luke 7:47 – "Whoever is forgiven much, loves much..."

Unwrapped in the Presence of God   127
    2 Corinthians 3:18 – "We... are being transformed... into his image..."

Grace with Skin On   129
    John 1:14 – "The Word became flesh... full of grace and truth."

The Gift I Keep Trying to Earn   131
    Galatians 3:3 – "After beginning by means of the Spirit, are you now trying to finish by means of the flesh?"

Even This, He Covers   133
    Isaiah 1:18 – "Though your sins are like scarlet, they shall be white as snow."

I'm Not Who I Was (But Grace Knew That Already)   135
    Philippians 1:6 – "He who began a good work in you..."

Songs Between the Storms: Selahs for the Soul

Sparrows & Thunder
Seeing God in the little and loud.

The God Who Counts Sparrows   139
  Matthew 10:29-31 - "Not one of them falls to the ground outside your Father's care."

He Moves in the Middle of Mayhem   141
  Psalm 29:3 - "The voice of the Lord is over the waters; the God of glory thunders..."

I'm Seen Even When I'm Small   143
  Genesis 16:13 - "You are the God who sees me..."

The Thunder Didn't Scare Him   145
  Job 37:5 - "God thunders wondrously with His voice..."

When Little Things Become Holy   147
  Zechariah 4:10 - "Do not despise these small beginnings..."

Heaven Is Louder Than the Storm   149
  Psalm 93:4 - "Mightier than the thunder... mightier than the breakers... is the Lord."

Tiny Miracles in Tired Places   151
  1 Kings 19:12 - "...the still small voice."

He Shows Up in the Shaking   153
  Hebrews 12:26-27 - "...so that what cannot be shaken may remain."

I Found God in the Details   155
  Luke 12:7 - "Even the hairs of your head are all numbered..."

The Ground Still Trembles, But I Don't   157
  Psalm 16:8 - "I will not be shaken..."

The Whisper After the Storm   159
  1 Kings 19:11-12 - "...but the Lord was not in the fire... and after the fire, a still small voice."

Songs Between the Storms: Selahs for the Soul

The Other Side of Silence

Coming out singing.

The Silence Broke First   163
Luke 1:64 – "Immediately his mouth was opened and his tongue set free..."

Now I Know What Joy Costs   165
John 16:22 – "Now is your time of grief, but I will see you again and you will rejoice..."

I Spoke Again, But Different   167
Isaiah 50:4 – "The Sovereign Lord has given me a well-instructed tongue..."

Peace That Didn't Need Permission   169
Philippians 4:7 – "The peace of God... will guard your hearts and minds..."

This Praise Has Scars   171
Psalm 40:2-3 – "He lifted me... put a new song in my mouth..."

The Sound of Joy Returning   173
Psalm 30:11 – "You turned my mourning into dancing..."

Nothing Missing But the Weight   175
James 1:4 – "...that you may be perfect and complete, lacking nothing."

The Answer Was Already in Me   177
Romans 8:11 – "The Spirit of him who raised Jesus from the dead dwells in you..."

I Don't Need the Whole Picture to Praise   179
Habakkuk 3:17-18 – "Yet I will rejoice in the Lord..."

The Quiet Has a New Meaning Now   181
Psalm 131:2 – "I have calmed and quieted my soul..."

I Still Sing (And Always Will)   183
Psalm 146:2 – "I will praise the Lord all my life..."

Selah Together: *A Group Discussion Guide*   188

Songs Between the Storms: Selahs for the Soul

Wounds & Whispers

This section is for the soul that has been bruised—
by betrayal, silence, exhaustion, or loss—
and is unsure whether God is still listening.

These poems sit in the ache of unspoken prayers and quiet suffering, but they do not stay there. They lean in close to the whispering God who collects every tear, holds every fragment, and speaks healing in the dark.

These are the Selahs for when you can't say much... but still want to be held.

Breath Prayer:
Inhale: "You are near."
Exhale: "Even when I can't speak."

Let your sigh become a prayer.
God hears what your voice cannot say.

When Tears Burn Quiet

"You have taken account of my wanderings; Put my tears in Your bottle. Are they not in Your book?"
— Psalm 56:8 (NASB)

My tears don't splash,
they smolder.
Hot silence leaking
from soul-fires I didn't start
but still must tend.

I whisper prayers with no punctuation,
no proper shape—
just smoke and fragments.
Still... You catch each drop.
Label them holy.

Bottle them like wine
for the day I sing again.

You see what others scroll past.
You sit in rooms no one else enters.
You know the burnt offerings
of breathless sobs
and the altar built
from what's left
after the storm left me.

I thought silence meant absence.
But even silence speaks
when it belongs to You.

Selah Reflection

There are tears no one sees. Cries we don't even have words for. But God keeps every single one—
not in pity, but as proof of divine nearness. When the fire of life consumes, He is the One who draws close with holy bottles and promises that nothing spilled in pain is wasted.

Spiritual Challenge

Don't rush past the ache. Sit long enough to let God collect what you cannot explain—
and trust that even your silence has sound in heaven.

Breath Prayer:
Inhale: "You are near."
Exhale: "Even when I can't speak."

Let your sigh become a prayer.
God hears what your voice cannot say.

Lament with No Return Address

"O Lord, You have searched me and known me... Even before a word is on my tongue, behold, O Lord, You know it altogether."
— Psalm 139:1,4 (ESV)

I mailed a prayer
with no stamp,
no name,
no return.

Just grief folded into
the corners of a sigh
and dropped into the wind,
half hoping You'd hear.

I didn't sign it
because pain made me forget
who I was.

But You knew.
You always know.
You read between the ache,
trace my trembling lines,
and respond without waiting
for my courage
to show its face.

You answer prayers
that never leave the chest.
You reply to silence
with mercy's breath.

Even when I forget
my address in You—
You never lose me.

Selah Reflection

Some prayers don't make it into words. But God reads sighs, interprets groans, and responds to spiritual mail that never got properly sealed. He does not need your strength to respond—only your surrender.

Spiritual Challenge

Write a short letter to God today with no edits—just raw honesty. Then let it go. He already knows, but the act of releasing helps you remember: you're still known, even when you're unsure of your voice.

Breath Prayer:
Inhale: "You are near."
Exhale: "Even when I can't speak."

Let your sigh become a prayer.
God hears what your voice cannot say.

Cracked Clay, Still Held
"But we have this treasure in jars of clay, to show that the surpassing power belongs to God and not to us."
— 2 Corinthians 4:7 (ESV)

I cracked
somewhere between
what I lost
and what I feared losing next.

My edges don't hold
like they used to.
Grace leaks.
Hope seeps slow.

But You—
You're the kind of Potter
who doesn't discard
what breaks.

You cup the shattered,
kiss the dust,
and call it still holy.

Not because I'm unbroken,
but because You
are unbending
in love.

I am both
the wound
and the wonder.

Still held.
Still Yours.

Selah Reflection

Being cracked doesn't disqualify you from being called. God's glory is not diminished by your fractures—
if anything, His light shines clearer through them. He specializes in holding what others deem hopeless.

Spiritual Challenge

Look at one place in your life that feels broken. Name it. Then declare over it: "This is still held by God.

Breath Prayer:
Inhale: "You are near."
Exhale: "Even when I can't speak."

Let your sigh become a prayer.
God hears what your voice cannot say.

When the Mirror Lies

"For now we see in a mirror, dimly, but then face to face. Now I know in part; then I shall know fully..."
— 1 Corinthians 13:12 (ESV)

The mirror told me
I was unworthy.
Too fractured to reflect
anything sacred.

It magnified the mess,
blurred the beauty,
spoke louder than grace
on days I felt small.

But You—
You don't look through glass.
You look through covenant.

You saw me before
I saw myself—
before pain clouded
my name,
before shame rewrote
my reflection.

And You whispered,
"Child, I made that frame.
It holds My glory.
Even dim, you shine."

Selah Reflection

The mirror doesn't always tell the truth. Especially when cracked by trauma, shame, or silence. But God doesn't need glass to see glory. He sees through grace—
and what He sees is good.

Spiritual Challenge

Stand in front of a mirror today. Say aloud: "I am not what the mirror says. I am who God made me to be." Repeat until your soul believes it louder than your eyes.

Breath Prayer:
Inhale: "You are near."
Exhale: "Even when I can't speak."

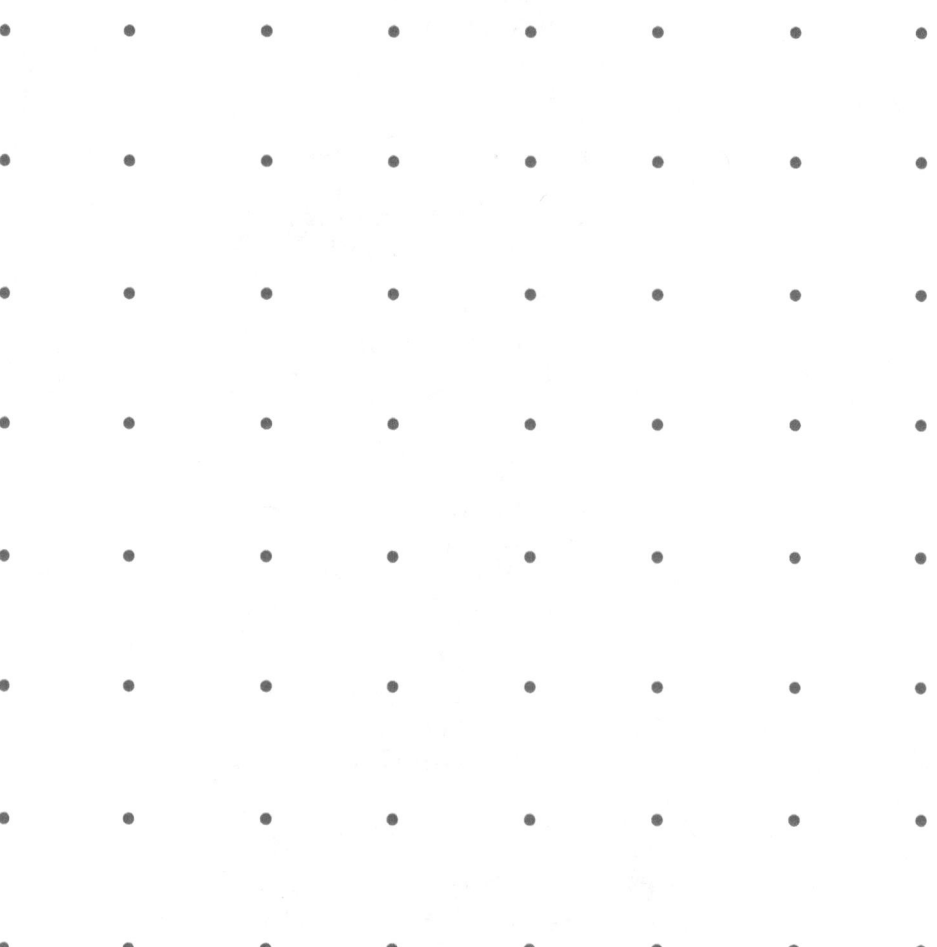

Let your sigh become a prayer.
God hears what your voice cannot say.

The Ache Between Amens

"Rejoice in hope, be patient in tribulation, be constant in prayer." — Romans 12:12 (ESV)

There's an ache
between the "Dear God"
and the "Amen."
A silence that swells
like an unanswered knock.

I speak.
I wait.
I wonder if heaven's line is busy
or if my voice
was too small
to register divine attention.

But still I pray.
Not because I always feel it,
but because my faith
was built in the waiting.

And somewhere in the ache,
You breathe.
Not loudly.
Not instantly.
But faithfully.
Tenderly.
Enough.

Selah Reflection

The space between your prayer and God's response can feel endless. But that in-between place is where your soul stretches and your faith finds new roots. God isn't ignoring you— He's growing you.

Spiritual Challenge

Think of a prayer you've repeated without clarity. Instead of asking again, sit in stillness and say: "Even here, You are enough." Let faith fill the ache.

Breath Prayer:
Inhale: "You are near."
Exhale: "Even when I can't speak."

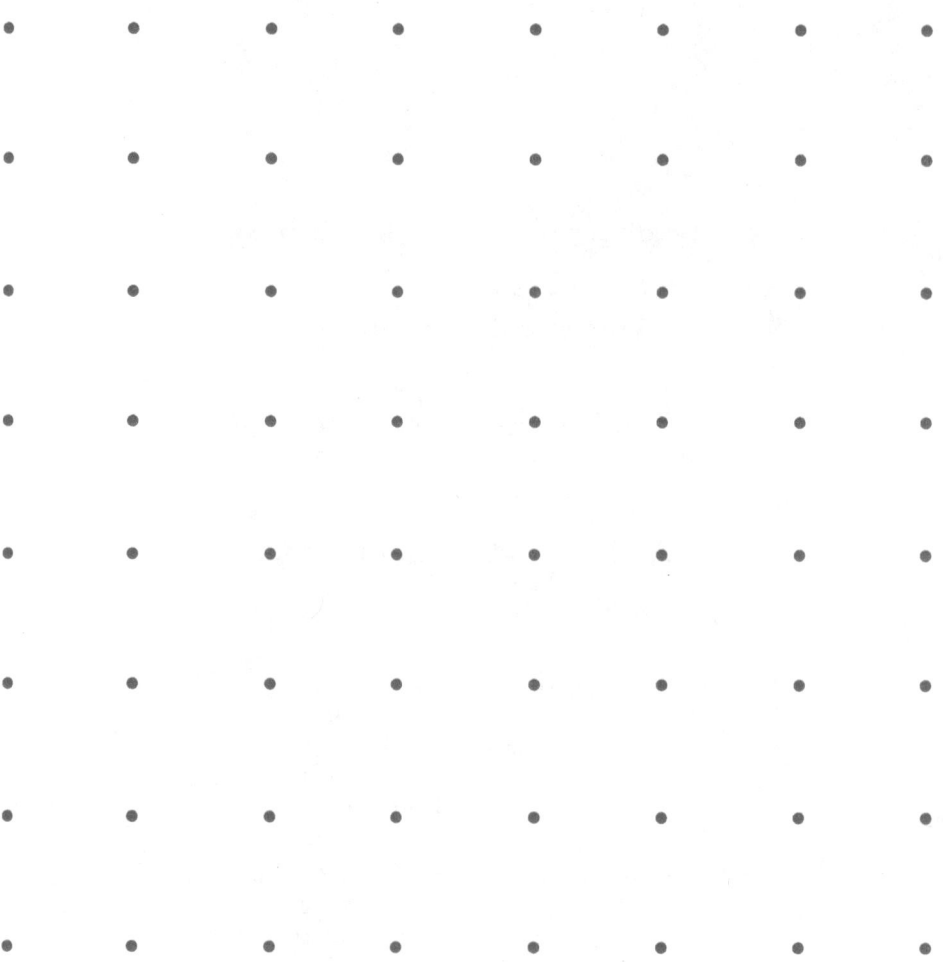

Let your sigh become a prayer.
God hears what your voice cannot say.

God Doesn't Flinch

"Even if my father and mother abandon me, the Lord will hold me close." — Psalm 27:10 (NLT)

I showed You the parts
I hid from others—
the jagged grief,
the angry blame,
the quiet questions
dressed in sarcasm.

I expected thunder.
Distance.
Judgment.

But You didn't flinch.
Didn't blink.
Didn't back away.

You came closer.
Took my rage in one hand,
my fear in the other,
and said,
"I'm still here."

Even when I cursed You
in confusion.
Even when I blamed You
for the silence.

Your love
didn't move.

Selah Reflection

God isn't afraid of your honesty. He doesn't flinch at your fears, your anger, or your grief. In fact, those raw places are often where He meets us most tenderly—
without rebuke, only love.

Spiritual Challenge

Say the thing you've been scared to say in prayer. Speak it fully. Then sit and listen. What does a God who doesn't flinch whisper back?

Breath Prayer:
Inhale: "You are near."
Exhale: "Even when I can't speak."

Let your sigh become a prayer.
God hears what your voice cannot say.

The Cry Behind My Eyes

"The Lord is near to the brokenhearted and saves the crushed in spirit." — Psalm 34:18 (ESV)

I didn't cry out loud—
I just stared.
Too tired to weep,
too numb to rage,
too practiced at pretending.

But my soul screamed
behind my eyes.
And You—
You heard that kind of cry.

You moved closer
without fanfare.
No lightning.

Just presence.
Just nearness.
Just You.

And somehow,
that was louder
than grief.

Selah Reflection

There are cries too deep for sound. But God hears the kind that live behind your eyes—
the silent sobs of the spirit. And He doesn't need volume to validate your pain.

Spiritual Challenge

Close your eyes today and simply whisper: "Come near." Trust that He already has.

Breath Prayer:
Inhale: "You are near."
Exhale: "Even when I can't speak."

Let your sigh become a prayer.
God hears what your voice cannot say.

I Named It Nothing

"He gives beauty for ashes, the oil of joy for mourning..."
— Isaiah 61:3 (NKJV)

I called it "nothing."
That loss.
That buried disappointment.
That dream I let rot in the corner.

I thought it didn't matter
because no one asked,
no one noticed,
and I didn't even cry.

But You searched the shadows
and found it.
Held it.
Named it valuable.

You don't throw away
what I forget to grieve.

You redeem what I dismiss.

Even my "nothings"
are worthy of resurrection.

Selah Reflection

We often bury pain too small to explain, thinking it doesn't deserve grief. But God resurrects forgotten losses. He's the only One who can turn overlooked wounds into living testimonies.

Spiritual Challenge

Write down something you've minimized or buried. Ask God to show you what He sees in it. Ask: "What are You resurrecting from this?"

Breath Prayer:
Inhale: "You are near."
Exhale: "Even when I can't speak."

Let your sigh become a prayer.
God hears what your voice cannot say.

Hands Too Tired to Lift

*"Moses' hands grew weary... so they held up his hands...
one on one side, and the other on the other side."
— Exodus 17:12 (ESV)*

My hands were made to praise
but some days
they barely lift off my lap.

The weight of this world
has turned them to stone,
too tired to reach,
too sore to clap,
too honest to fake it.

But You—
You send help.
A phone call.
A quiet friend.
A verse I didn't expect.

And I learn again
that praise doesn't always sound like shouting.
Sometimes,
it sounds like breathing
when I thought I couldn't.

Selah Reflection

Worship isn't measured by volume or posture—
it's measured by surrender. Even exhausted hands, lifted by others, are still a holy offering.

Spiritual Challenge

Reach out to someone today with this message: "I don't have much strength, but I could use someone to hold my hands up." Let community carry you.

Breath Prayer:
Inhale: "You are near."
Exhale: "Even when I can't speak."

Let your sigh become a prayer.
God hears what your voice cannot say.

The Silence After the Shout

"For thus said the Lord God, the Holy One of Israel, 'In returning and rest you shall be saved; in quietness and in trust shall be your strength.'" — Isaiah 30:15 (ESV)

I shouted.
Loud prayers.
Bold declarations.
Tears that dared You to move.

And when I was spent...
nothing.

Just stillness
and the slow drip
of holy hush.

I thought You didn't care.
But You were waiting—
not for the shout,
but for the stillness after it.

You met me
where words ran out
and trust had to take over.

Sometimes, the silence
is the answer.

Selah Reflection

After the shout, God often whispers. He waits for the storm of our emotions to quiet, not because He's punishing us—but because He wants to speak where only peace can echo.

Spiritual Challenge

Spend five minutes in absolute silence. No phone. No noise. Just your breath and God. Listen—
not for an answer, but for His nearness.

Breath Prayer:
Inhale: "You are near."
Exhale: "Even when I can't speak."

Let your sigh become a prayer.
God hears what your voice cannot say.

I Still Belong

"The Spirit Himself bears witness with our spirit that we are children of God." — Romans 8:16 (NKJV)

I haven't been consistent.
Haven't prayed like I used to.
Skipped the songs,
ignored the stirrings.

I thought maybe I'd forfeited
my seat at the table.
But then—
You sent the whisper.

Not of guilt,
but of belonging.

You reminded me
that family doesn't forget blood.
And covenant
doesn't break easy.

I still belong.
Even limping.
Even quiet.
Even last to show up.

You saved my seat.

Selah Reflection

God doesn't cross your name off His list when you wander. Grace is not performance-based. It's presence-based. And His presence still has a place for you.

Spiritual Challenge

Say aloud: "I still belong." Even if it feels untrue, speak it. Let the Spirit confirm what your feelings forget.

Songs Between the Storms: Selahs for the Soul

Waiting in the Wind

This section explores the tension of delay, longing, and trust when everything is still—
or seems like it. These poems hold space for those in seasons of waiting: for healing, answers, justice, clarity, or the storm to pass.

Breath Prayer:
Inhale: "I will wait..."
Exhale: "...because You are worth it."

You don't have to see the movement to believe God is working.

Held by a Thread

"He has made everything beautiful in its time. Also, he has put eternity into man's heart..." — Ecclesiastes 3:11 (ESV)

I'm dangling
by a thread of hope—
thin,
fraying,
but somehow
still holding.

I've stopped asking,
"How long?"
and started asking,
"Will it matter when it comes?"

But even the thread
is grace.

Because You never said
I had to feel strong
to be safe—
only tethered.

Even when time mocks me,
You anchor me to beauty
I can't see yet.

And when I finally touch it—
I'll understand
why You made me wait.

Selah Reflection

Sometimes hope doesn't feel like a roar. It feels like a whisper tied to a single thread. But God is in the thread. And what He is weaving will one day reveal the beauty that now feels hidden.

Spiritual Challenge

Don't measure your faith by strength. Measure it by who you're holding on to. Whisper today: "Even this thread leads to You."

Breath Prayer:
Inhale: "I will wait..."
Exhale: "...because You are worth it."

You don't have to see the movement to believe God is working.

The Clock That Doesn't Move

"A thousand years in your sight are like a day that has just gone by..." — Psalm 90:4 (NIV)

I've watched the same minute
on the clock
for what feels like months.

Life moves
for everyone else—
but my time
sits still
and stares back
like it's mocking me.

I tap,
I shake,
I plead.

And You say:
"Time belongs to Me,
but you belong to eternity."

You aren't slow.
You're steady.
You aren't punishing.
You're preparing.

Even paused clocks
can be prophetic.

Selah Reflection

Waiting distorts time. But God is not bound by seconds or years. What feels stagnant to you may be sacred pacing from Him. He doesn't delay from disinterest—
but from intentional love.

Spiritual Challenge

Find one clock today and sit with it for five quiet minutes. As it ticks, say, "I trust Your timing, Lord—
even when mine feels louder."

Breath Prayer:
Inhale: "I will wait..."
Exhale: "...because You are worth it."

You don't have to see the movement to believe God is working.

Still Doesn't Mean Stuck

"The Lord will fight for you; you need only to be still."
— Exodus 14:14 (NIV)

Stillness isn't the enemy—
it's the invitation
I keep declining.

Because moving
feels like control,
and silence
feels like surrender
I didn't choose.

But You aren't stuck.
You're steady.
You aren't absent.
You're acting—
just not the way I would.

The sea doesn't split
until the stillness
settles into trust.

So I stop
fighting silence
and start watching
for miracles.

Selah Reflection

We often mistake God's stillness for distance. But stillness is where clarity often comes—
and where God moves most powerfully. Still doesn't mean forgotten. It means "wait and watch."

Spiritual Challenge

Choose one moment today to pause fully. No noise. No fixing. Just stillness. Breathe and say: "I'm not stuck—
I'm still, and He is fighting for me."

Breath Prayer:
Inhale: "I will wait..."
Exhale: "...because You are worth it."

You don't have to see the movement to believe God is working.

When the Promise Feels Like a Lie

"For the vision is yet for an appointed time... though it tarry, wait for it; because it will surely come, it will not tarry."
— Habakkuk 2:3 (KJV)

I believed You.
The first time.

The second.
Even the seventh.

But now the promise
feels like
a fairy tale for people
with better faith
or cleaner hands.

I want to trust—
but the delay
feels personal.

Still,
something in me
won't let go.
Maybe it's holy stubbornness.
Or maybe it's You
refusing to lie.

Even slow promises
are still true
if they come from a faithful mouth.

So I'll hold the echo
until the voice returns.

Selah Reflection

God's promises don't expire with time. Delay does not mean deception. When the promise feels distant, trust the integrity of the Promiser more than the speed of the process.

Spiritual Challenge

Speak aloud the promise you're still waiting for. Then say, "Though it tarries, I will wait—because He does not lie."

Breath Prayer:
Inhale: "I will wait..."
Exhale: "...because You are worth it."

You don't have to see the movement to believe God is working.

Windless Worship

"But the hour is coming, and is now here, when the true worshipers will worship the Father in spirit and truth..."
— John 4:23 (ESV)

I worshipped
with no breeze,
no goosebumps,
no breakthrough.

The room felt hollow,
the notes heavy,
the silence too loud.

But still I sang.
Still I bowed.
Still I offered
what didn't feel enough.

And You received it
like incense
lit without fire.

Because true worship
isn't measured
by how I feel—
but by Who I trust.

Even when the wind doesn't blow,
You are still worthy.

Selah Reflection

Worship in the wind is easy. Worship in the stillness is sacrifice. When we sing without answers, lift hands without movement—that's when trust becomes worship.

Spiritual Challenge

Worship today without seeking a feeling. Just give Him your presence. Say: "Even when nothing moves—my praise still rises."

Breath Prayer:
Inhale: "I will wait…"
Exhale: "…because You are worth it."

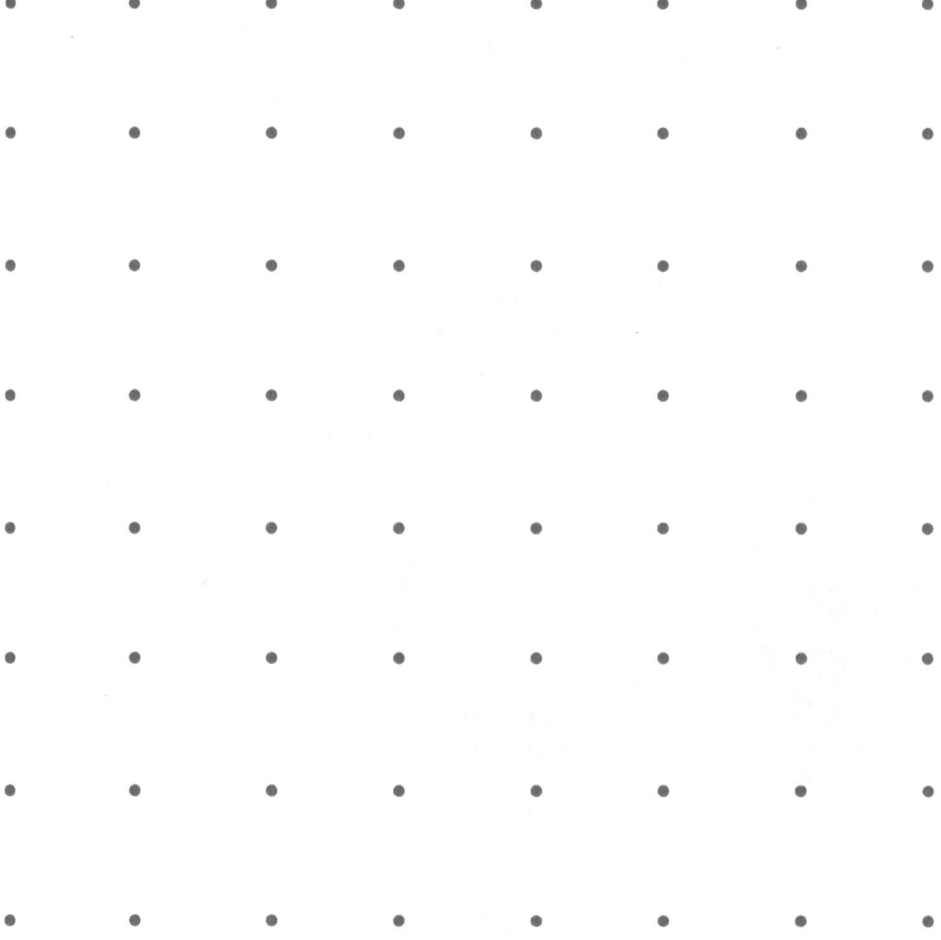

You don't have to see the movement to believe God is working.

Nothing Is Happening (And That's Something)

"But those who wait on the Lord shall renew their strength..."
— Isaiah 40:31 (NKJV)

I can't see the roots growing.
I can't feel the healing happening.
I can't track the grace
moving quietly beneath the surface.

So I say,
"Nothing is happening."
But You say,
"Everything is shifting."

Strength doesn't always feel
like motion—
sometimes it's just
the refusal to give up.

Sometimes the silence
is the seed's way
of becoming a tree.

So I wait.
Not in despair,
but in quiet agreement
with what I cannot yet see.

Selah Reflection

Waiting doesn't mean wasting. In stillness, God renews you. Even when nothing seems to be happening, heaven is not idle. Growth begins underground.

Spiritual Challenge

Say: "I may not see it yet, but You are working beneath the surface." Choose trust, even in what looks like nothing.

Breath Prayer:
Inhale: "I will wait..."
Exhale: "...because You are worth it."

You don't have to see the movement to believe God is working.

I Prayed, Then Waited, Then Doubted

"Immediately the father of the child cried out and said, 'I believe; help my unbelief!'" — Mark 9:24 (ESV)

I prayed bold
at first—
like thunder
in the desert.
But days passed,
and my voice shrank
to a whisper
so soft
I wasn't sure
You still heard it.
Then came doubt—
not loud,
but slow,
like fog that blurs
the lines between faith
and fear.
And yet,
even doubt
has a door
You still walk through.
You didn't need
a perfect prayer—
just an honest one.
And mine
was cracked,
but still open.

Selah Reflection

Faith isn't erased by doubt—it is revealed through it. Jesus responded to the man who believed and struggled to believe. Your hesitation doesn't scare God. He honors your honesty.

Spiritual Challenge

Whisper, "I believe, but help my unbelief." Then rest— He responds to both.

Breath Prayer:
Inhale: "I will wait..."
Exhale: "...because You are worth it."

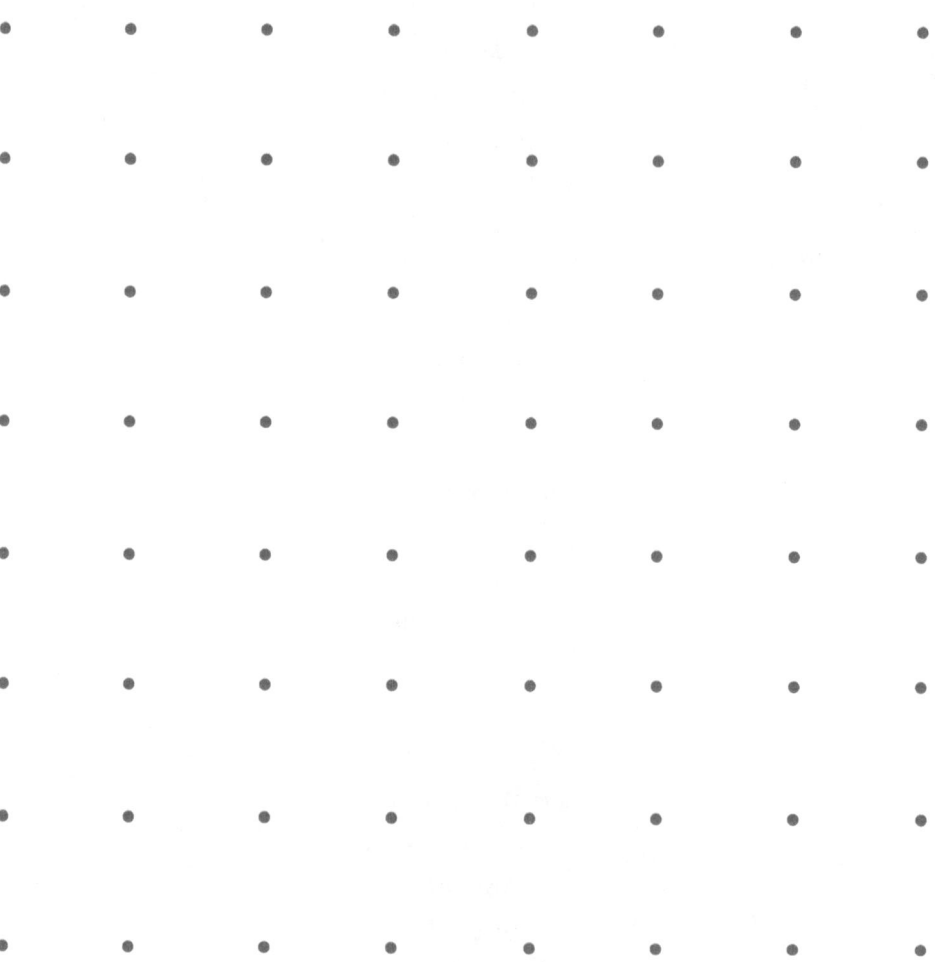

You don't have to see the movement to believe God is working.

The Weight of Waiting
"Wait for the Lord; be strong, and let your heart take courage; wait for the Lord!" — Psalm 27:14 (ESV)

Waiting is a weight
I didn't ask to carry.
It drags on my soul,
settles in my spine,
wraps around my prayers
like iron vines.
People say,
"Be patient."
They mean well.
But they don't feel
this ache
in my chest.
Still—
I wait.
Not because I want to,
but because hope
refuses to release me.
And maybe
this weight
isn't crushing me—
maybe it's shaping me.
Maybe it's making room
for what's coming.

Selah Reflection
Waiting can feel heavy. But the weight isn't meant to break you—it's meant to build your capacity. Strength is not the absence of heaviness, but the courage to carry it in trust.

Spiritual Challenge
Breathe deeply. Say: "Lord, give me strength for what I carry and faith for what I cannot yet see."

Breath Prayer:
Inhale: "I will wait..."
Exhale: "...because You are worth it."

You don't have to see the movement to believe God is working.

Tired of Hoping

"Hope deferred makes the heart sick, but a longing fulfilled is a tree of life."
— Proverbs 13:12 (NIV)

Hope used to feel
like sunlight—
bright,
certain,
near.
Now it feels
like a flicker
in fog,
a candle burning low
on both ends.
I'm tired
of waiting
for what I thought
You promised.
Tired of feeling
like I believed
too soon
or too big.
But something holy
keeps my eyes lifted—
maybe it's mercy,
maybe it's muscle memory.
Either way,
I still scan the horizon
for the first sign
of joy returning.

Selah Reflection

It's okay to admit you're tired of hoping. Even hope has a cost. But God does not despise your fatigue—He meets you there. And He will turn even faint hope into new strength.

Spiritual Challenge

Say aloud: "I'm tired, but I haven't let go." Then ask God to rekindle what's flickering.

Breath Prayer:
Inhale: "I will wait..."
Exhale: "...because You are worth it."

You don't have to see the movement to believe God is working.

Stillness Is a Song
"He will quiet you with His love, He will rejoice over you with singing."
— Zephaniah 3:17 (NKJV)

Stillness is not silence—
it's a different kind of music.

A soft hum
beneath the noise
where love sings
without needing words.

It is the sacred hush
between sorrow and strength,
the pause before the promise,
the melody hidden
in the breath
of God.

I once thought joy
required volume,
but now I hear
that stillness
has its own harmony—
and You're the Composer.

You're singing over me
even now.

Selah Reflection
God's love doesn't always come with thunder—
it often comes with quiet. When we stop straining to hear answers, we start to hear the music of His presence. Stillness is a sacred song.

Spiritual Challenge
Find five minutes to sit in complete quiet. Don't ask. Don't explain. Just listen for love.

Breath Prayer:
Inhale: "I will wait..."
Exhale: "...because You are worth it."

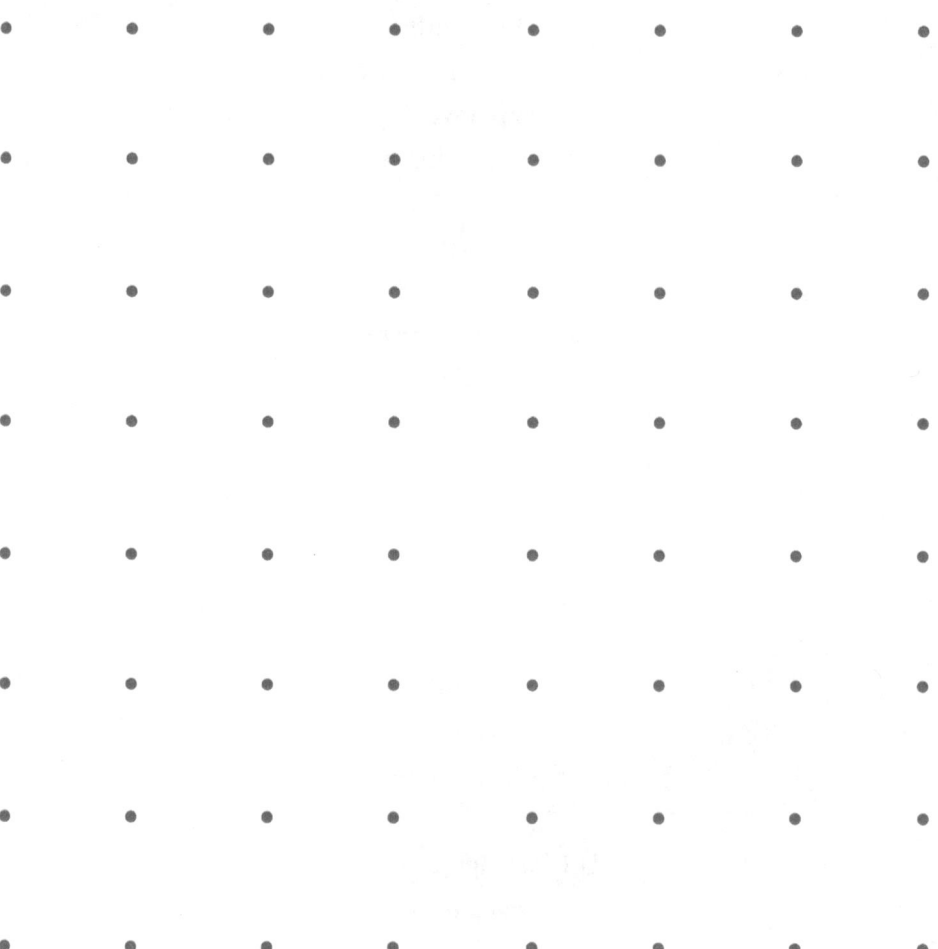

You don't have to see the movement to believe God is working.

If the Wind Never Comes

"But even if He does not, we want you to know... we will not serve your gods..."
— Daniel 3:18 (NIV)

I've been waiting
for the wind—
the shift,
the sign,
the sudden deliverance.
But what if it doesn't come?
What if the breakthrough
never breaks,
and the answer
never arrives
wrapped in light?
Will I still stay?
Will I still trust
the One who sat with me
in the waiting
even if He never moves
the mountain?
Faith is not proven
by the outcome,
but by the anchor.
And my soul,
bruised as it is,
has decided to stay tethered
even if the wind
never blows.

Selah Reflection

The deepest faith is not found in the miracle—it's found in the even if. When we choose to stay with God, even without results, we show the world what real trust looks like.

Spiritual Challenge

Pray: "Even if You don't move how I want—still, I will worship You." Let that become your offering today.

Songs Between the Storms: Selahs for the Soul

Bitter Waters & Better Promises

This section is for those who've tasted life's bitterness—disappointment, betrayal, unanswered prayers, hard detours—and are wrestling with whether to believe again. Inspired by Exodus 15, where the bitter waters of Marah were made sweet, this section explores how God meets us in the bitter and invites us to trust again.

Breath Prayer:
Inhale: "You are still good."
Exhale: "Even in the bitter."

*What once wounded you may
become the place God whispers the loudest.*

Bitterness in My Mouth

"When they came to Marah, they could not drink its water because it was bitter... and the Lord showed him a tree. He threw it into the water, and the water became sweet."
— Exodus 15:23,25 (CSB)

I expected relief—
found bitterness.
I came thirsty,
but the water cut my tongue
with memory,
with mourning.

This wasn't supposed to be like this.
Didn't You lead me here?

But then—
You didn't change the place.
You changed the taste.

Not by denying the pain
but by planting redemption in it.

A tree.
A shadow of another tree
You would hang on.

And bitter became holy.

Not because it was easy—
but because You touched it.

Selah Reflection

Bitterness does not mean God abandoned you. Sometimes the waters He brings us to are bitter—so He can show us that redemption isn't about escape, but transformation. And He still heals what hurts when we trust Him to touch it.

Spiritual Challenge

Name something that still tastes bitter in your life. Then ask: "Lord, what tree are You placing in these waters?"

Breath Prayer:
Inhale: "You are still good."
Exhale: "Even in the bitter."

*What once wounded you may
become the place God whispers the loudest.*

This Wasn't the Plan

"A person's heart plans his way, but the Lord determines his steps." — Proverbs 16:9 (CSB)

This wasn't the way
I mapped it.
I had the route highlighted,
the milestones pre-pinned,
the prayers already answered
in my imagination.

Then came the detour.

Loss.
Delay.
A door slammed
with no explanation.

And I wanted to scream,
"This wasn't the plan!"

But You were never working
from my blueprint.
You were writing a better story
with rougher roads
and deeper wells.

Maybe the plan didn't fail—
maybe it just grew
into something holy.

Selah Reflection

We cling tightly to our plans—but growth often lives in the interruptions. God doesn't abandon your vision; He purifies it through detours you never expected. He's not rewriting the promise, just deepening it.

Spiritual Challenge

List three things that didn't go as planned. Ask: "God, how are You still leading in these?"

Breath Prayer:
Inhale: "You are still good."
Exhale: "Even in the bitter."

*What once wounded you may
become the place God whispers the loudest.*

The Prayer I Prayed in Pieces

"The Spirit Himself intercedes for us with groanings too deep for words." — Romans 8:26 (ESV)

It wasn't eloquent.
Wasn't even whole.
Just fragments of grief
scattered between sighs.

I prayed it
in pieces—
one breath here,
one tear there.

And You—
You gathered every sliver.
Held the parts I couldn't name.
Translated silence
into sacred language.

You answered
not with thunder,
but with presence.

Not with solution,
but with stillness.

Because even when my prayer
was incomplete,
Your love was not.

Selah Reflection

Not every prayer comes out whole. And God never asks it to. His Spirit hears even the groans, the fragments, the wordless aches. He prays with you—when all you can do is breathe.

Spiritual Challenge

Take a moment and breathe deeply three times. As you exhale, say: "You hear even this."

Breath Prayer:
Inhale: "You are still good."
Exhale: "Even in the bitter."

*What once wounded you may
become the place God whispers the loudest.*

I Forgave, but I Still Remember

"Be kind to one another, tenderhearted, forgiving one another, as God in Christ forgave you." — Ephesians 4:32 (ESV)

I said the words.
Meant them, mostly.
Let go of the fist
I kept in my chest.

But memory lingers
like smoke
after the fire is gone.

I see their face
and feel the bruise again—
not as pain,
but as proof
that healing still has layers.

You never asked me
to forget.
Just to forgive.

And maybe remembering
isn't a failure—
maybe it's a scar
turned testimony.

Not a wound reopened,
but a mercy remembered.

Selah Reflection

Forgiveness isn't amnesia. God doesn't ask us to forget—it's okay to remember, as long as the memory leads to mercy, not resentment. Your scars aren't signs of failure. They're signs of grace working.

Spiritual Challenge

Say this aloud: "I remember—but I release. Again and again, I choose mercy." Let it be your rhythm, not your regret.

Breath Prayer:
Inhale: "You are still good."
Exhale: "Even in the bitter."

What once wounded you may
become the place God whispers the loudest.

Why Did You Let It Hurt?

"Lord," Martha said to Jesus, "if You had been here, my brother would not have died." — John 11:21 (CSB)

I didn't want theology.
I wanted presence.
A hand to hold
when the world
broke open.

I said it softly—
"If You had been here..."
because pain can't always
dress itself in praise.

But You didn't rebuke me.
You wept with me.

You knew
the resurrection was coming,
but You still sat
in my sorrow.

And that—
that was the miracle
before the miracle.

Not power.
Not timing.
But love
that doesn't run
from grief.

Selah Reflection

God is not offended by your questions. He doesn't withdraw when you ask "why." In fact, Jesus wept before He healed—because love doesn't skip lament. He's not just the God of resurrection, but of presence in pain.

Spiritual Challenge

Ask the question you've been avoiding. Then listen. God may not answer with "why," but He will always answer with Himself.

Breath Prayer:
Inhale: "You are still good."
Exhale: "Even in the bitter."

*What once wounded you may
become the place God whispers the loudest.*

I Want to Believe Again
"Do not fear, only believe."— Mark 5:36 (ESV)

Disappointment
has a way
of draining the soul.
I used to believe
with boldness.
I had the kind of faith
that filled rooms
and silenced doubt.
But now—
I flinch
before hoping.
Because what if
it breaks again?
Still, something in me
aches to believe.
To trust
without trembling.
And You whisper,
"Start small.
I'm not asking for a mountain—
just a mustard seed."
So I gather my fragments
and offer them up.
Faith, again.

Even if it's fragile.

Selah Reflection
Faith doesn't have to be flawless—it just has to return. If you've stopped believing, God is still welcoming you back. Start small. One whisper of trust is enough for Him to work with.

Spiritual Challenge
Pray: "God, I want to believe again. Even if it's weak, make it real." Let that be the first step back into trust.

Breath Prayer:
Inhale: "You are still good."
Exhale: "Even in the bitter."

**What once wounded you may
become the place God whispers the loudest.**

The Promise Has Teeth

"For all the promises of God in Him are Yes, and in Him Amen, to the glory of God through us." — 2 Corinthians 1:20 (NKJV)

I used to think
Your promises were soft—
like lullabies
or clouds I couldn't catch.

But now I know:
they have teeth.

They bite into the lies I believed.
They tear through fear
with truth too strong
to dissolve in delay.

They hold.
Even when I don't.
Even when I scream,
cry,
walk away.

Your promises stay put.
Rooted.
Roaring.
Refusing to let me forget
that covenant doesn't fade
in the dark.

Selah Reflection

God's promises are not fragile. They don't vanish in storms. They are sharper than doubt, stronger than delay, and more enduring than our emotions. They will outlast your bitterness.

Spiritual Challenge

Declare out loud: "God's promises are stronger than my pain." Write down one promise to carry with you this week.

Breath Prayer:
Inhale: "You are still good."
Exhale: "Even in the bitter."

*What once wounded you may
become the place God whispers the loudest.*

Don't Let Bitterness Preach

"See to it that no bitter root grows up to cause trouble and defile many." — Hebrews 12:15 (NIV)

Bitterness has a sermon.
It preaches in silence,
echoes in isolation,
and convinces me
that protection
means never feeling again.

It tells me
You can't be trusted.
That softness
is dangerous.
That cynicism is wisdom
with armor on.

But Your truth
whispers louder.

It says healing
hurts,
but hardening
kills.

And I don't want
my bitterness
to disciple anyone.

Not even me.

Selah Reflection

Bitterness can become your theology if you let it. But God calls us to uproot it—not ignore it—so that it won't choke out joy or sour the witness of your life.

Spiritual Challenge

Ask: "What lie has bitterness taught me?" Write the opposite truth beside it. Let grace interrupt the sermon bitterness has been preaching.

Breath Prayer:
Inhale: "You are still good."
Exhale: "Even in the bitter."

*What once wounded you may
become the place God whispers the loudest.*

He Met Me at Marah

"Oh, taste and see that the Lord is good; Blessed is the man who trusts in Him!" — Psalm 34:8 (NKJV)

I didn't meet You
in the miracle—
I met You
at Marah.

At the bitter spring
where faith felt thin
and healing felt cruel.

You didn't rush me.
Didn't shame me
for gagging on grief.

You just sat beside me,
offering sweetness
not from the water,
but from Your presence.

And somehow,
what was unbearable
became holy.

Not because it stopped hurting—
but because You hurt with me.

Selah Reflection

God doesn't only show up in breakthroughs. Sometimes He meets you in bitterness—not to fix it right away, but to sit with you in it. His presence is the sweetness you didn't expect.

Spiritual Challenge

Pause and ask: "Where is God sitting with me in what I want Him to change?" Let gratitude grow even before relief comes.

Breath Prayer:
Inhale: "You are still good."
Exhale: "Even in the bitter."

*What once wounded you may
become the place God whispers the loudest.*

It Was Sweet All Along

"You intended to harm me, but God intended it for good..."
— Genesis 50:20 (NIV)

Looking back—
what I thought
was punishment
was planting.

What I thought
was silence
was strategy.

You weren't being cruel—
You were being close.
I just didn't know
how hidden goodness
can wear bitter clothes.

The taste was sharp,
but the fruit?
Still sweet.

It didn't feel good,
but it worked good.

And now I see—
what broke me
built something holy.

Selah Reflection

Often, we can't see God's goodness until we look back. What felt bitter at first may turn out to be the soil of the sweetest growth in your life.

Spiritual Challenge

Reflect: What painful moment has produced unexpected fruit in your life? Thank God for using what was meant to break you to bless you instead.

Breath Prayer:
Inhale: "You are still good."
Exhale: "Even in the bitter."

*What once wounded you may
become the place God whispers the loudest.*

Better Than I Asked For

"Now to Him who is able to do exceedingly abundantly above all that we ask or think…" — Ephesians 3:20 (NKJV)

I asked for a fix—
You gave me a future.

I asked for a detour—
You gave me direction.

I asked for the pain to pass—
You made it purposeful.

I thought You were ignoring me.
Turns out,
You were preparing something
I hadn't even thought to request.

You're the God
who listens
to my prayers
but answers
with better ones.

And now—
my faith has grown teeth,
my peace has roots,
and my joy
tastes sweeter
than I ever imagined.

Selah Reflection

Sometimes God says no to what we ask because He's saying yes to what we didn't know we needed. He's not ignoring you—He's exceeding you.

Spiritual Challenge

Write a prayer that starts, "Thank You for the thing I didn't know to ask for…" Let wonder replace bitterness.

Songs Between the Storms: Selahs for the Soul

Midnight Melodies

This section sings in the dark. It's for the soul that knows nighttime all too well—those 3 a.m. battles with anxiety, loneliness, shame, or waiting. But these poems don't just survive the night—they find a song inside it. Inspired by Paul and Silas singing in prison (Acts 16), these *midnight melodies* remind us that worship isn't reserved for daylight, and light isn't the only thing that makes God visible.

These Selahs speak to hearts that may be trapped, tired, or trembling in the dark—and still, somehow, singing.

Breath Prayer:
Inhale: "Even here..."
Exhale: "...I still sing."

Your midnight song doesn't need to be loud—
it just needs to be real.

When the Song is a Whisper

"By day the Lord commands his steadfast love, and at night his song is with me..." — Psalm 42:8 (ESV)

It wasn't a loud praise.
Just a hum,
barely a note,
cracked between breaths
in a room too dark to see.

But it was still a song.

Because even broken hallelujahs
count in heaven.

Even when the voice trembles,
even when the hands won't lift—
the whisper still rises
and finds You.

You don't require volume,
just honesty.
You don't need harmony,
just heart.

So I sing.
Soft.
Shaky.
Sure.
And somehow,
You sing back.

Selah Reflection

In the night, songs don't need to be perfect to be powerful. God meets the whisper like He meets the roar. Your quiet praise still moves heaven.

Spiritual Challenge

Whisper a worship lyric before bed tonight. Let it be the last thing your spirit hears before sleep.

Breath Prayer:
Inhale: "Even here..."
Exhale: "...I still sing."

Your midnight song doesn't need to be loud—
it just needs to be real.

The Chains Didn't Break First

"About midnight Paul and Silas were praying and singing hymns to God... and suddenly there was a great earthquake..."
— Acts 16:25-26 (ESV)

They didn't wait
for the chains to fall
before they sang.

They sang with them.
With the bruises.
With the pain.
With the iron still wrapped
around their freedom.

Because worship
wasn't a response—
it was resistance.

They lifted their voice
in defiance of the dark,
and the prison
couldn't hold the praise.

Maybe breakthrough doesn't come
before the song.
Maybe it is the song.

Selah Reflection

God doesn't always remove the chains before we worship. But when we choose to praise while still bound, we declare where our freedom truly comes from.

Spiritual Challenge

Don't wait for the problem to end—worship now. Say: "Even here, even now, You're still worthy."

Breath Prayer:
Inhale: "Even here..."
Exhale: "...I still sing."

*Your midnight song doesn't need to be loud—
it just needs to be real.*

I Sing So I Don't Surrender

"But I will sing of Your power; yes, I will sing aloud of Your mercy in the morning..." — Psalm 59:16 (NKJV)

I sing,
not because I feel strong—
but because I feel surrounded.

I sing to remind my fear
that I still have a God.

When the night closes in
and nothing makes sense,
my song
becomes my stand.

Even off-key,
even low,
even through tears.

This is not noise.
This is warfare.
This is worship.

I sing
so I don't surrender
to the dark
that doesn't own me.

Selah Reflection

Worship isn't always celebratory. Sometimes it's survival. Every note you sing in the dark declares that despair won't have the final word.

Spiritual Challenge

Turn on a worship song tonight and sing one verse, even if you're hurting. Let the act of singing become your strength.

Breath Prayer:
Inhale: "Even here..."
Exhale: "...I still sing."

*Your midnight song doesn't need to be loud—
it just needs to be real.*

Silence Is Still a Sound

"For God alone my soul waits in silence; from him comes my salvation." — Psalm 62:1 (ESV)

I thought silence
meant You left.
That the quiet
was a punishment,
a door slammed shut
on my prayers.

But now I'm learning—
silence isn't absence.
It's invitation.
It's where You wait
to be found without noise.

Stillness is not empty.
It's sacred.

You don't always answer out loud.
Sometimes You just breathe
near enough
that I feel peace
settle into the corners of me.

And that's sound enough.

Selah Reflection

Silence is not spiritual failure. It is space for the Spirit to whisper. Trust that God may be saying more in the quiet than He could in a thousand words.

Spiritual Challenge

Sit in silence for five minutes today. No asking. Just listening. Let stillness become sacred.

Breath Prayer:
Inhale: "Even here…"
Exhale: "…I still sing."

Your midnight song doesn't need to be loud—
it just needs to be real.

Midnight Feels Like Forever

"Because of the Lord's great love we are not consumed... His mercies are new every morning." — Lamentations 3:22–23 (NIV)

Midnight stretches.
It doesn't keep time—
it keeps weight.
Heavy hours
that fold into each other
like shadows with no edges.

I count minutes,
but they don't answer.
I pray,
but the room stays still.

Is morning still coming?

Then—
a flicker of mercy
in the dark.
Not loud,
but enough.

A reminder:
I'm not consumed.
Not alone.
Not forgotten.

Even in forever midnight,
You are faithful.

Selah Reflection

Darkness distorts time. But God's mercy is never late—even when the clock feels cruel. If you're still breathing, morning is coming.

Spiritual Challenge

Say aloud: "This night will not last forever. Mercy is already on its way."

Breath Prayer:
Inhale: "Even here…"
Exhale: "…I still sing."

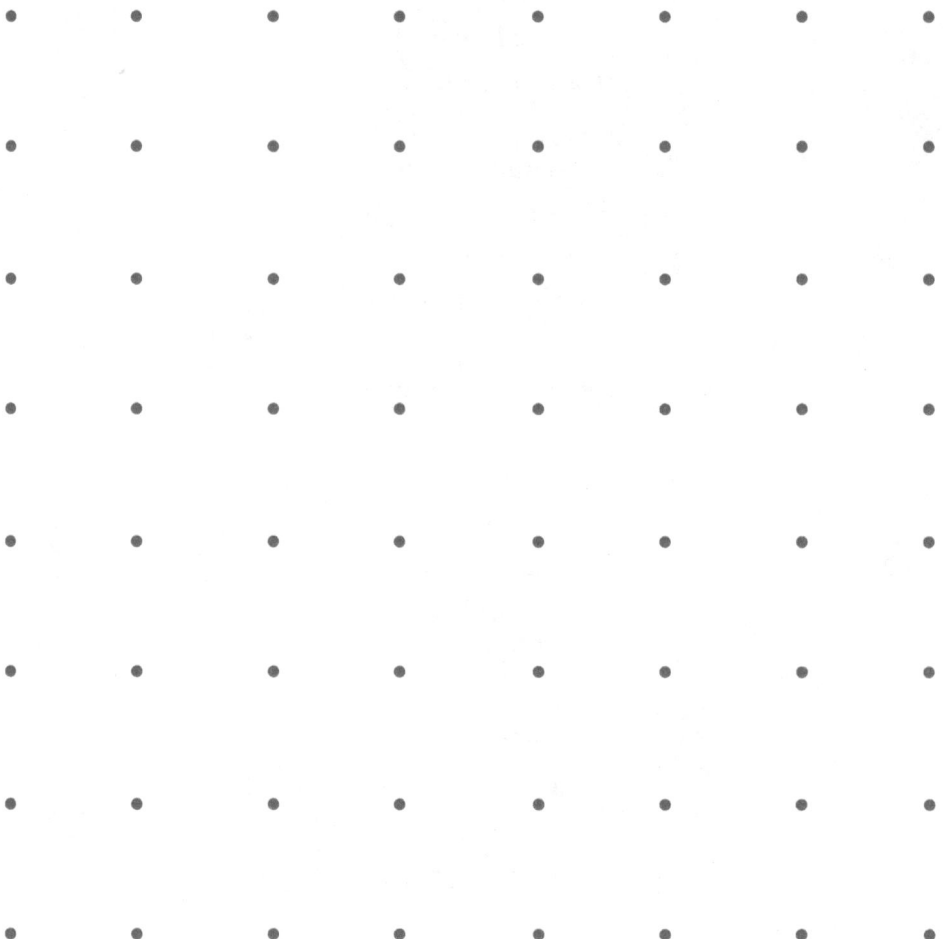

*Your midnight song doesn't need to be loud—
it just needs to be real.*

My Song Is Off-Key, But It's Mine

"Make a joyful noise to the Lord, all the earth!" — Psalm 100:1 (ESV)

I don't always sing in tune.
My melody stumbles.
My rhythm forgets
how praise is supposed to sound.

But I sing anyway.
Because this song
is mine.
Forged in the furnace.
Shaped in the shadows.

And I know—
You're not listening
for perfection.
You're listening
for presence.

Every cracked note,
every broken lyric,
still makes heaven lean in.

Because I'm not performing—
I'm surviving.

And survival
sounds like song.

Selah Reflection

God is not grading your worship. He's receiving your heart. Even the most broken song becomes beautiful when it's sung in truth.

Spiritual Challenge

Sing something today—anything. Even just a hum. Let your soul know it still has a song.

Breath Prayer:
Inhale: "Even here..."
Exhale: "...I still sing."

Your midnight song doesn't need to be loud—
it just needs to be real.

The Night I Prayed Without Words

"The Spirit Himself intercedes for us with groanings too deep for words." — Romans 8:26 (ESV)

There was no language
for that night.
Just the heaviness
of breath too thick
to rise as prayer.

No words.
Just a pillow soaked with ache
and a soul too tired
to perform faith.

But You were there.
Not waiting for me to speak—
already speaking for me.

You turned my sighs
into sacred sentences.
My tears into testimony.
My stillness into sanctuary.

And somehow,
without a word,
You heard everything.

Selah Reflection

Prayer doesn't require perfect phrasing. God knows the language of silence. When you can't speak, the Spirit speaks for you. He's fluent in brokenness.

Spiritual Challenge

Sit with your journal open today. Even if you can't write a word, let the empty page become your prayer. Trust that God fills in the blanks.

Breath Prayer:
Inhale: "Even here..."
Exhale: "...I still sing."

*Your midnight song doesn't need to be loud—
it just needs to be real.*

There's a Hallelujah in the Hurt

"I will bless the Lord at all times; His praise shall continually be in my mouth." — Psalm 34:1 (NKJV)

I didn't think
"hallelujah"
could live
next to heartbreak.

But pain
has a way
of hollowing space
for deeper praise.

Not loud.
Not bright.
But honest.

A hallelujah
with a limp.
With trembling hands.
With tears that still fall
between verses.

You didn't ask for pretty.
You asked for real.

And in the hurt,
my praise found a home.

Selah Reflection

Praise in pain is the most powerful worship. Not because it ignores the hurt, but because it refuses to be silenced by it. That kind of hallelujah shakes heaven.

Spiritual Challenge

Say: "Hallelujah—even here." Let that be your declaration today, even if your voice is shaking.

Breath Prayer:
Inhale: "Even here..."
Exhale: "...I still sing."

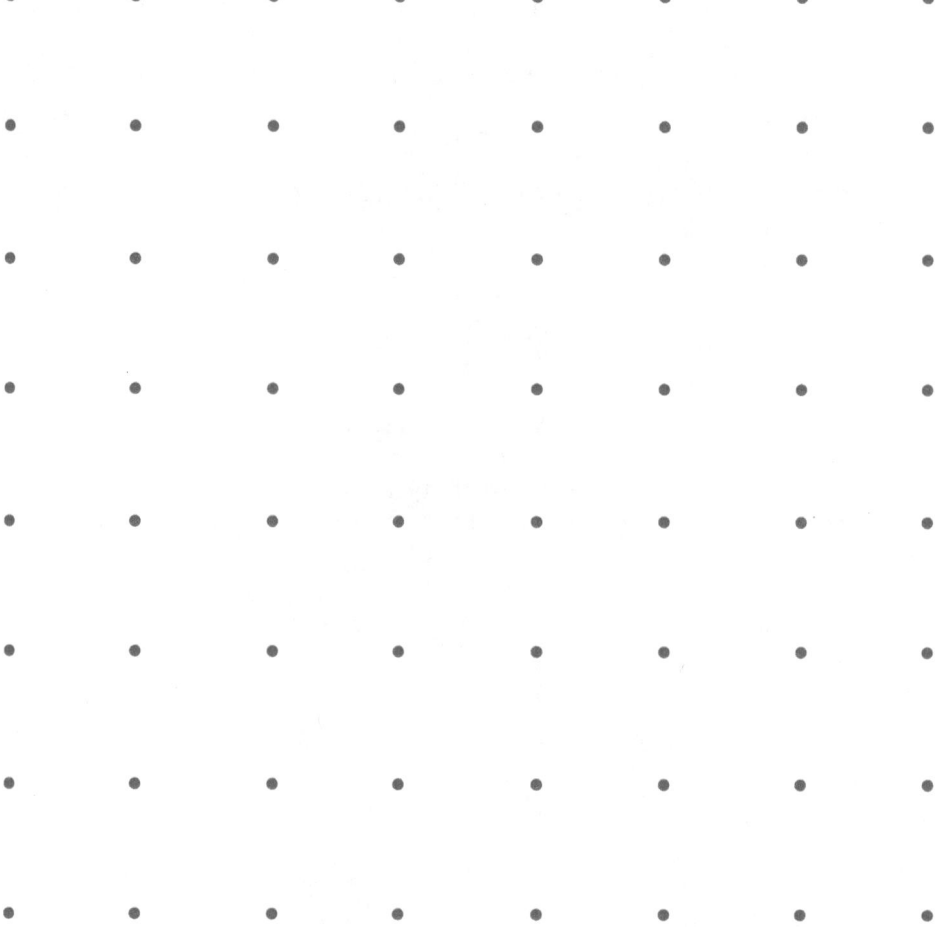

Your midnight song doesn't need to be loud—
it just needs to be real.

Before the Earthquake, There Was Worship

"About midnight Paul and Silas were praying and singing hymns to God... and suddenly there was a great earthquake."
— *Acts 16:25-26 (ESV)*

Before the shaking—
there was singing.

Before the doors flew open—
there were two wounded men
raising broken voices
into cold prison air.

No promises of release.
No guarantees of rescue.
Just worship.

They didn't wait
for the miracle.
They became the miracle.

Their praise
was the prophecy
of freedom coming.

And when the earth responded,
it was just catching up
to what heaven
had already heard.

Selah Reflection

Breakthrough often begins before the shift. Praise prepares the ground. Even when nothing changes around you, something changes in you when you worship.

Spiritual Challenge

Before you ask for the breakthrough, sing anyway. Let praise lead the earthquake.

Breath Prayer:
Inhale: "Even here..."
Exhale: "...I still sing."

Your midnight song doesn't need to be loud—
it just needs to be real.

Dark Doesn't Mean Defeated

"The light shines in the darkness, and the darkness has not overcome it." — John 1:5 (ESV)

The night is long,
but it is not lord.

The dark
presses in—
but it cannot
possess.

You shine
without needing spotlights.
You move
without needing to be seen.

And just because I can't trace You
doesn't mean I've been abandoned.

The enemy wants me
to mistake quiet
for loss,
shadows
for surrender.

But my soul remembers—
dark doesn't mean defeated.

Light has already won.
Even here.

Selah Reflection

The presence of darkness doesn't mean the absence of God. The light of Christ shines in the night, not just after it. You are not losing—you are still lit by His love.

Spiritual Challenge

Say aloud: "This darkness is not my ending. Light has already won." Let that become your nighttime creed.

Breath Prayer:
Inhale: "Even here..."
Exhale: "...I still sing."

*Your midnight song doesn't need to be loud—
it just needs to be real.*

This Night Will Not Last Forever

"Weeping may endure for a night, but joy comes in the morning." — Psalm 30:5 (NKJV)

It's hard to believe in morning
when the night feels
like a sentence
without parole.

Grief stretches the hours.
Pain blurs the minutes.
And hope feels
like someone else's story.

But I've lived long enough
to see the sun
chase sorrow back
into the shadows.

And if morning came once,
it can come again.

Even now—
as tears find their way
into my pillowcase—
I rehearse the promise:

This night
will not
last forever.

Selah Reflection

No matter how endless it feels, the night does have boundaries. Joy will come. It may not erase the pain, but it will shine enough light for you to see love again.

Spiritual Challenge

Before bed, say: "Joy is coming." Repeat it until your soul starts to believe it again.

Songs Between the Storms: Selahs for the Soul

The Weight of Grace

Grace is often described as light and freeing—but sometimes, grace is *heavy*. It humbles us. It unmasks us. It calls us to live forgiven when we'd rather hide, and to receive mercy when we feel unworthy. This section explores the strange pressure grace puts on the soul—the weight of being loved so deeply that you can't earn it, and the call to extend that same grace to others.

These poems are for those wrestling with what it means to be forgiven... and what it means to forgive.

Breath Prayer:
Inhale: "I receive..."
Exhale: "...what I could never earn."

Let grace carry what you keep trying to fix.

When Grace Feels Too Heavy to Hold

"Where sin abounded, grace abounded much more."
— Romans 5:20 (NKJV)

Some days, grace feels like a blanket.
Other days—
like a boulder I'm not strong enough to carry.

I know You've forgiven me,
but it overwhelms me—
the size of it.
The reach.
The memory of what I was
and the miracle of still being called "loved."

I drop it often.
Try to adjust it.
Make it smaller,
so I don't have to feel so exposed
under something so generous.

But You remind me:
grace isn't mine to manage.
It's Yours to give.
And mine to receive—
again, and again.

Selah Reflection

Sometimes grace feels too big because we're still trying to prove we deserve it. But grace isn't something you carry to earn—it carries you, even when you fall beneath its weight.

Spiritual Challenge

Whisper: "Even this, You've covered." Let that be the posture you stand in today.

Breath Prayer:
Inhale: "I receive..."
Exhale: "...what I could never earn."

Let grace carry what you keep trying to fix.

This Mercy Makes Me Tremble

"Let us then with confidence draw near to the throne of grace, that we may receive mercy..." — Hebrews 4:16 (ESV)

I walked in afraid.
Hands full of excuses,
heart hiding in shame.

But You met me
with mercy that didn't flinch—
that didn't shame,
didn't shrink back.

And suddenly,
what I deserved
stood face-to-face
with what I received.

Not wrath.
Not punishment.
But embrace.

And I trembled.
Not from fear—
but from love
so holy,
so undeserved,
I didn't know whether to cry
or bow.

So I did both.

Selah Reflection

Mercy isn't weak. It's powerful enough to disarm what judgment cannot. If it makes you tremble, that's not a flaw—that's worship rising from the shock of being fully known and fully loved.

Spiritual Challenge

Take a moment today to say thank You for the mercies you've received but never fully acknowledged.

Breath Prayer:
Inhale: "I receive…"
Exhale: "…what I could never earn."

Let grace carry what you keep trying to fix.

I Don't Deserve This (And That's the Point)

*"For by grace you have been saved through faith...
it is the gift of God."* — *Ephesians 2:8 (ESV)*

I keep trying to earn it—
rehearsing my goodness
like it's currency
to exchange for kindness.

But grace doesn't play by those rules.
It bankrupts my pride
and blesses me anyway.

This love—
it doesn't wait for me
to meet the standard.
It redefines the standard
by stepping into my mess
and calling it worthy
of redemption.

I don't deserve this.
And I never will.
But maybe that's not a reason
to resist it—
maybe that's the reason
I should worship.

Selah Reflection

Grace wouldn't be grace if you deserved it. Stop striving. Let the undeserved gift become your undeserved freedom.

Spiritual Challenge

Pray: "I let go of earning. I receive what I can't repay." Let grace do its perfect, unbalanced work.

Breath Prayer:
Inhale: "I receive..."
Exhale: "...what I could never earn."

Let grace carry what you keep trying to fix.

Forgiven Doesn't Mean Forgotten

"I, even I, am He who blots out your transgressions for My own sake; and I will not remember your sins."
— Isaiah 43:25 (NKJV)

I still remember
what I did—
the words,
the silence,
the running.

But You?
You say You don't.

Not because You can't,
but because You choose not to.

You see the stain,
but call it clean.
You know the chapter,
but don't quote it back.

Forgiveness doesn't mean
erasing the past—
it means You refuse
to let it define me.

And when I look back,
it's not shame I see,
but grace standing guard
at the door I'll never enter again.

Selah Reflection

God's forgiveness is not forgetfulness—it's freedom. He remembers you, not your sin. You don't have to keep rehearsing what heaven already released.

Spiritual Challenge

Speak this aloud: "That version of me is not who I am." Then thank God for His divine forgetfulness.

Breath Prayer:
Inhale: "I receive…"
Exhale: "…what I could never earn."

Let grace carry what you keep trying to fix.

The Shame Grace Refused to Carry
"There is therefore now no condemnation for those who are in Christ Jesus."
— *Romans 8:1 (ESV)*

Shame came knocking
with a full report—
dates, names,
every wrong I hoped
was buried.

But grace stood in the doorway
and said,
"This house is no longer under that law."

I wanted to invite shame in—
because it felt like justice.

But You wouldn't let me.
You carried the guilt,
but not the shame.

Because shame lies.
It keeps me tied
to chains You already broke.

And Your grace
refused to carry
what no longer belongs on me.

Selah Reflection
Shame is not repentance. Shame keeps you stuck in a prison grace already unlocked. God doesn't use shame to grow you—He uses mercy to free you.

Spiritual Challenge
Write down something shame keeps repeating. Then cross it out and write: "Grace carried this. I don't have to."

Breath Prayer:
Inhale: "I receive…"
Exhale: "…what I could never earn."

Let grace carry what you keep trying to fix.

The Grace I Can't Repay

"Her many sins have been forgiven—as her great love has shown."
— Luke 7:47 (NIV)

I want to pay it back.
For all the mercy.
For all the mornings You stayed
when I walked away.

But grace doesn't ask for repayment.
It just asks for response.

So I give You this—
a heart cracked open,
hands not full of gold
but surrender.

I give You the kind of worship
that flows from the woman
who broke her jar
at Your feet.

Not because she was holy—
but because she was forgiven.

And that kind of love
can't be measured.
Only poured out.

Selah Reflection

You'll never be able to pay God back—and He never asked you to. Grace invites worship, not repayment. Love Him like someone who's been rescued.

Spiritual Challenge

Break your "jar" today. Do something generous, vulnerable, or bold in worship—not to earn grace, but to respond to it.

Breath Prayer:
Inhale: "I receive…"
Exhale: "…what I could never earn."

Let grace carry what you keep trying to fix.

Unwrapped in the Presence of God

"We all, with unveiled face, beholding the glory of the Lord, are being transformed... into His image..." — 2 Corinthians 3:18 (ESV)

I used to come wrapped tight—
in apology,
in performance,
in carefully chosen words
to make me seem
less broken than I felt.
But You never asked
for the costume.
You asked for me.
The trembling.
The tangled.
The true.
And slowly,
Your presence unwrapped me—
layer by layer—
until all that was left
was raw worship
and a soul not hiding.

And You called that
glory.

Not because I was flawless—
but because I was finally
seen.

Selah Reflection

God doesn't transform what we pretend to be. His presence unwraps us so He can shape what's real. Being seen by Him is not your undoing—it's your becoming.

Spiritual Challenge

Pray uncovered today. No filter. No preamble. Just truth. Let His presence do the unwrapping.

Breath Prayer:
Inhale: "I receive…"
Exhale: "…what I could never earn."

Let grace carry what you keep trying to fix.

Grace with Skin On

"The Word became flesh and dwelt among us... full of grace and truth."
—John 1:14 (NKJV)

You didn't send a scroll.
You came Yourself.
Full of grace
that walked,
bled,
wept,
healed.
Grace with skin on.
Not theory—
person.
Not concept—
compassion.
You sat with the messy.
Touched the untouchable.
Ate with the ashamed.
And called it holy work.
Grace isn't soft.
It's sacrificial.
It doesn't just cover—
it carries.
And when I needed it most,
You didn't just extend it—
You became it.
For me.

Selah Reflection

Grace isn't an idea. It's a Person. Jesus showed us that grace walks into mess, sits in pain, and holds what others would cast away. That's what love with skin looks like.

Spiritual Challenge

Ask: Who needs grace with skin on today? Be the kindness that shows up like Christ did.

Breath Prayer:
Inhale: "I receive…"
Exhale: "…what I could never earn."

Let grace carry what you keep trying to fix.

The Gift I Keep Trying to Earn

"After beginning by means of the Spirit, are you now trying to finish by means of the flesh?" — Galatians 3:3 (NIV)

You gave me grace
like a gift.
Wrapped,
unearned,
freely mine.

And I...
tried to earn it anyway.
Tried to do enough,
be enough,
prove I was worth
the wrapping.

But grace doesn't work like wages.
It doesn't grow with striving
or shrink with struggle.

It just is.

A gift that breathes.
A love that stays.
A kindness I can't perform into
or out of.

So I stop hustling
and start receiving—
again.

Selah Reflection

You can't finish in your own strength what God began in grace. The pressure to earn will suffocate the freedom Christ already gave. Let yourself rest in what's already yours.

Spiritual Challenge

Say aloud: "I don't have to earn what Jesus already finished." Then take a deep breath and rest in that truth.

Breath Prayer:
Inhale: "I receive…"
Exhale: "…what I could never earn."

Let grace carry what you keep trying to fix.

Even This, He Covers

"Though your sins are like scarlet, they shall be as white as snow..." — Isaiah 1:18 (NKJV)

There are things I haven't told anyone—
mistakes I renamed
so I wouldn't have to mourn them.

But You knew.
You always knew.

And still—
You covered it.

Not with denial,
but with blood.
Not with silence,
but with sacrifice.

Even this,
the thing I swore disqualified me—
You looked at it
and said,
"Mine to carry."

And I no longer hide.
Because what I once buried
is now buried in grace.

Covered.
Completely.

Selah Reflection

There is no sin so deep that grace won't cover it. You don't have to hide what Jesus already carried to the cross. If He says "even this," then even this.

Spiritual Challenge

Whisper it in your heart: "Even this, You've covered." Let those four words be your freedom prayer today.

Breath Prayer:
Inhale: "I receive…"
Exhale: "…what I could never earn."

Let grace carry what you keep trying to fix.

I'm Not Who I Was (But Grace Knew That Already)

"He who began a good work in you will complete it..."
— Philippians 1:6 (NKJV)

I still catch glimpses
of the old me—
the one who ran,
the one who lied,
the one who wore shame like skin.

But she doesn't get
the final word.

Because grace
started a work in me
that even my worst days
can't undo.

And while I'm still becoming,
grace isn't surprised.
It never was.

It saw the end
before I saw the beginning.

And the same hands
that held me in my lowest
are shaping me
into something holy.

Still flawed.
Still forming.
Still free.

Selah Reflection

You're not who you were. And even if you're not yet who you will be, grace isn't done. You're in process, and grace is patient.

Spiritual Challenge

Say: "I am not who I was—and grace is still working." Let that be your permission to keep growing.

Songs Between the Storms: Selahs for the Soul

Sparrows & Thunder

This section explores how God shows up in both the *smallest details* and the *loudest storms*. From unnoticed sparrows to crashing thunder, the poems in this section honor the paradox of a God who is both intimate and infinite—gentle enough to see your silent cry, and powerful enough to shake the foundations of your life for good.

These Selahs are for the soul learning to trust God's hand in both the *whisper* and the *whirlwind*.

Breath Prayer:
Inhale: "You see the sparrow..."
Exhale: "...and You see me."

God speaks through thunder and through stillness.
Listen for both.

The God Who Counts Sparrows

"Are not two sparrows sold for a penny? Yet not one of them will fall to the ground outside your Father's care... So don't be afraid; you are worth more than many sparrows."
— Matthew 10:29-31 (NIV)

I thought I was too small
to be seen.
Too quiet
to be counted.
Too easily missed
by a God so big.

But then I read
You count sparrows—
creatures most people forget.

Not one falls
without Your knowing.
Not one sings
without You listening.

So if You care
for wings that flutter unseen,
surely You care
for the weight I carry
in silence.

I am not invisible.
I am intimately held.

And that truth
has wings of its own.

Selah Reflection

God doesn't miss small things. He counts sparrows, hairs, tears, and whispered prayers. If He sees the birds, He surely sees you.

Spiritual Challenge

Say aloud: "You see me." Let that simple truth interrupt every lie of invisibility today.

Breath Prayer:
Inhale: "You see the sparrow…"
Exhale: "…and You see me."

God speaks through thunder and through stillness.
Listen for both.

He Moves in the Middle of Mayhem

"The voice of the Lord is over the waters; the God of glory thunders, the Lord thunders over the mighty waters."
— Psalm 29:3 (NIV)

Chaos doesn't cancel God—
sometimes it reveals Him.

While waves crash
and winds scream,
His voice
thunders above them.

Not drowned out,
but defining.

He doesn't wait
for peace to show up
before He speaks.
He speaks into the storm
and makes it obey.

Mayhem is not the absence of God—
it's often the setup
for His glory to be heard louder
than anything else around you.

The world shakes.
But His voice?
It still reigns.

Selah Reflection

God isn't waiting for your life to settle before He speaks. His power doesn't avoid chaos—it commands it. Listen closely; His voice still rules the storm.

Spiritual Challenge

In one area of life that feels chaotic, pray: "Speak louder than this storm, Lord." Then listen.

Breath Prayer:
Inhale: "You see the sparrow..."
Exhale: "...and You see me."

*God speaks through thunder and through stillness.
Listen for both.*

I'm Seen Even When I'm Small

"She gave this name to the Lord who spoke to her: 'You are the God who sees me.'" — *Genesis 16:13 (NIV)*

I wasn't in the spotlight.
Didn't get the call.
Wasn't invited to the table
where decisions are made.

But You still saw me.

In the back row.
In the kitchen.
In the moment no one else noticed.

And like Hagar
in the wilderness,
I found water
not just for my thirst—
but for my soul.

Because You don't need
a crowd to care.
You don't need
a stage to stop.

You are the God
who sees
the ones the world forgets.

And that's enough for me
to keep walking.

Selah Reflection

God sees you when no one else claps. When no one else calls. His gaze is not reserved for the great—it rests lovingly on the forgotten.

Spiritual Challenge

Where do you feel overlooked? In that place, whisper: "You see me here too, Lord." Let that be your comfort today.

Breath Prayer:
Inhale: "You see the sparrow..."
Exhale: "...and You see me."

God speaks through thunder and through stillness.
Listen for both.

The Thunder Didn't Scare Him

"God thunders wondrously with his voice; he does great things that we cannot comprehend." — Job 37:5 (ESV)

The sky broke open.
Thunder rolled like judgment.
And I braced myself—
thinking maybe You would too.

But You didn't flinch.
Didn't hide.
Didn't leave.

You stood in the storm,
unmoved.

And that's when I realized—
the thunder doesn't threaten You.
It obeys You.

What scares me
still serves You.
And if You're not afraid,
maybe I can breathe deeper
while the storm rages.

Not because it's quiet—
but because You are sovereign
in the sound.

Selah Reflection

God is not alarmed by what alarms you. He's Lord over the thunder, not victim to it. His calm is your courage.

Spiritual Challenge

Say: "If the thunder doesn't move You, it won't move me either." Repeat it when fear comes knocking.

Breath Prayer:
Inhale: "You see the sparrow..."
Exhale: "...and You see me."

God speaks through thunder and through stillness.
Listen for both.

When Little Things Become Holy

"Do not despise these small beginnings, for the Lord rejoices to see the work begin..." — Zechariah 4:10 (NLT)

It didn't look like much—
the small step,
the quiet yes,
the tear no one else saw fall.

But You rejoiced in it.

Because You're the God
who anoints the unnoticed.
Who multiplies mustard seeds
and calls crumbs
the start of a feast.

You make the small
sacred.

So I won't wait
until it's big
to call it blessed.

Even this
beginning—
broken, quiet, slow—
is holy ground.

Selah Reflection

God delights in your small starts. Don't measure your faith by size—measure it by surrender. He sees what you began in secret and calls it sacred.

Spiritual Challenge

Write down one small thing you've done or offered to God. Say: "This matters to You." Then keep going.

Breath Prayer:
Inhale: "You see the sparrow..."
Exhale: "...and You see me."

God speaks through thunder and through stillness.
Listen for both.

Heaven Is Louder Than the Storm

"Mightier than the thunder of the great waters... the Lord on high is mighty."
— Psalm 93:4 (NIV)

The storm has a voice—
sharp, echoing,
filling the sky with noise.

But Heaven speaks too.
Not to compete—
but to overrule.

You don't need to shout
to be louder.
Your authority doesn't tremble
when thunder comes.

It commands it.

And when my life
feels overtaken by noise,
I will lean in—
not to the storm,
but to the stillness
that follows Your Word.

Because You're louder
even in a whisper.

Selah Reflection
The storm has volume, but God has authority. His Word has the final say. Don't fear the noise—tune your soul to the voice that speaks peace into it.

Spiritual Challenge
In a moment of stress, pause and say: "Heaven is louder." Let that truth still the storm inside you.

Breath Prayer:
Inhale: "You see the sparrow..."
Exhale: "...and You see me."

God speaks through thunder and through stillness.
Listen for both.

Tiny Miracles in Tired Places

"After the earthquake a fire, but the Lord was not in the fire; and after the fire a still small voice." — 1 Kings 19:12 (NKJV)

I expected fire.
I waited for thunder.
I begged for something big
to wake me out of this weariness.

But You whispered.

Not because You were far,
but because You were that close.
And the miracle
wasn't the volume—
it was the fact
that You still spoke
into my exhaustion
with gentleness.

You didn't need a spectacle.
You just needed
my stillness.

And there,
in my tiredness,
a tiny miracle unfolded—
quiet
but undeniable.

Selah Reflection

God often moves in subtle ways when we're the most weary. Don't miss the small miracles because you're looking for loud ones. His whisper is just as holy.

Spiritual Challenge

List one "small mercy" from this week—something quiet but meaningful. That's your miracle. Let it encourage you.

Breath Prayer:
Inhale: "You see the sparrow..."
Exhale: "...and You see me."

God speaks through thunder and through stillness.
Listen for both.

He Shows Up in the Shaking

"Once more I will shake not only the earth but also the heavens… so that what cannot be shaken may remain." — Hebrews 12:26–27 (ESV)

Everything shook.
Plans, people, places—
all fell from the shelves of certainty.

I thought the shaking
was the end.
But You called it the beginning.

Because what remains
after the shaking
is what matters most.

You didn't come
to comfort the clutter—
You came to clear it.

You didn't stop the shaking—
You stood inside it.

And somehow,
the ground held
because grace was beneath me
the whole time.

Selah Reflection

God doesn't always stop the shaking. Sometimes He allows it—so false security falls away and the unshakable truth remains. Let Him do holy work in the tremble.

Spiritual Challenge

Ask: "What is falling away—and what is staying?" Trust God to reveal the foundation beneath your fears.

Breath Prayer:
Inhale: "You see the sparrow..."
Exhale: "...and You see me."

God speaks through thunder and through stillness.
Listen for both.

I Found God in the Details

"Even the hairs of your head are all numbered."
— Luke 12:7 (ESV)

I used to think
God only moved in moments
loud enough
to make headlines.

But then I noticed—
You were in the tiny things.

The green light
when I needed it.
The friend who called
right on time.
The verse
I wasn't looking for
but found anyway.

You're not just the God
of mountains and miracles.
You're the God
of cracked mugs,
quiet laughter,
and whispered reminders
that I'm seen.

I didn't miss You.
You met me
in the details.

Selah Reflection

God is in the ordinary. He pays attention to what we overlook—because that's what love does. Don't underestimate the sacred in the small.

Spiritual Challenge

Notice one "little" thing today and thank God for it. Let gratitude anchor you to His presence.

Breath Prayer:
Inhale: "You see the sparrow..."
Exhale: "...and You see me."

God speaks through thunder and through stillness.
Listen for both.

The Ground Still Trembles, But I Don't

"I have set the Lord always before me; because He is at my right hand, I shall not be shaken." — Psalm 16:8 (NKJV)

Everything under me
shifted.
What I trusted cracked.
What I counted on
crumbled.

But I didn't fall.

Not because I'm strong—
but because You are steady.

I felt the tremble,
heard the rumble,
watched the pieces drop.

But my peace?
Still standing.

Because when the Lord
is the anchor,
the quake can't cancel
what's been secured
by grace.

The ground shook.
I didn't.

And that's the miracle.

Selah Reflection

Stability doesn't come from stillness around you—it comes from the God within you. When everything trembles, your anchor in Christ holds firm.

Spiritual Challenge

Pray: "Lord, be my unshakable place." As you go through your day, notice where His peace steadies you.

Breath Prayer:
Inhale: "You see the sparrow..."
Exhale: "...and You see me."

God speaks through thunder and through stillness.
Listen for both.

The Whisper After the Storm

"And after the fire came a still small voice."
— 1 Kings 19:12 (NKJV)

The fire passed.
The wind died down.
The earthquake settled into silence.

And then—
You whispered.

Not to impress me.
Not to overwhelm me.
But to remind me
that presence
doesn't require power.

You were there
all along,
waiting for the noise to leave
so You could speak
soft enough
that my soul had to lean in.

The storm was loud—
but You were louder
in the quiet.

And I finally heard You.

Selah Reflection

God often waits until the chaos quiets before He speaks—not because He was absent, but because He wanted you to come close. His whisper is where your healing begins.

Spiritual Challenge

Sit in silence for two minutes. Then pray: "I'm listening, Lord." Don't fill the space—just wait for the whisper.

Songs Between the Storms: Selahs for the Soul

The Other Side of Silence

This section is a sacred exhale. After the storm, after the silence, after the wrestling—there is something new. These poems are about *what happens when the waiting ends*, when the voice returns, when praise breaks through pain. But this isn't a flashy victory—
it's quiet strength, holy relief, and joy that's been tested by fire.

These Selahs are songs sung by someone who *knows* what silence feels like, and now sings with deeper reverence because of it.

Breath Prayer:
Inhale: "The silence has ended."
Exhale: "My soul still sings."

You made it through.
Let your praise be shaped by everything you survived.

The Silence Broke First

"Immediately his mouth was opened and his tongue set free, and he began to speak, praising God." — Luke 1:64 (NIV)

It wasn't the miracle
that broke the silence.
It was the praise.

Before the answer was explained,
before the crowd understood—
worship filled the air
like breath returning.

I had been quiet too long.
Not just mute—
wounded.
Waiting.

But when it was time,
my silence broke first.

Not because I had it all figured out—
but because I finally knew
who was worthy.

Even before the "why" came,
my praise came out like a flood
I forgot was dammed up.

And it was holy.

Selah Reflection

Sometimes praise comes before clarity. When silence breaks open, let worship be your first sound—not explanation, not defense. Just awe.

Spiritual Challenge

Say aloud: "Before I understand, I'll still worship." Let your voice lead the breakthrough.

Breath Prayer:
Inhale: "The silence has ended."
Exhale: "My soul still sings."

You made it through.
Let your praise be shaped by everything you survived.

Now I Know What Joy Costs

"So with you: now is your time of grief, but I will see you again and you will rejoice, and no one will take away your joy." —
John 16:22 (NIV)

Joy costs more now.
Not because it's rare—
but because I know
what preceded it.

I've wept enough
to understand
the strength it takes
to smile.

I've lost enough
to cherish laughter
like communion.

And now,
when joy returns,
I don't waste it.

I hold it slow.
Honor it.

Let it teach me
how to dance again
with reverence.

Because now I know—
joy is not cheap.
It's fought for.
And once it's yours,
it's yours forever.

Selah Reflection

Joy isn't always loud—it's often forged in sorrow and worn like armor. When you've cried enough, even a small smile is sacred.

Spiritual Challenge

Pause and remember: What has joy cost you? Thank God that what cost so much can never be taken from you again.

Breath Prayer:
Inhale: "The silence has ended."
Exhale: "My soul still sings."

You made it through.
Let your praise be shaped by everything you survived.

I Spoke Again, But Different

"The Sovereign Lord has given me a well-instructed tongue, to know the word that sustains the weary." — Isaiah 50:4 (NIV)

When I found my voice again,
I didn't use it the same.

The pain shaped my words—
softer, slower,
more like balm
than blade.

Before, I spoke to be heard.
Now, I speak to heal.

The silence taught me
how powerful a whisper can be—
how sacred it is
to say something
that carries God's breath.

I still speak.
But now my words
remember their weight.

And grace
sits behind every syllable.

Selah Reflection

After silence, speech can become sacred. Let your words carry healing—not noise. You don't have to say much to say something holy.

Spiritual Challenge

Today, speak one sentence that lifts someone. Let your words be an offering of grace.

Breath Prayer:
Inhale: "The silence has ended."
Exhale: "My soul still sings."

You made it through.
Let your praise be shaped by everything you survived.

Peace That Didn't Need Permission

"And the peace of God, which surpasses all understanding, will guard your hearts and minds through Christ Jesus." — Philippians 4:7 (NKJV)

It didn't ask to enter.
Didn't knock.
Didn't wait for conditions
to be perfect.

It just showed up—
this peace
that had no reason
but had every right.

I was still waiting on answers.
Still walking with questions.
But suddenly,
peace took up residence
like a warrior,
guarding my joy
against despair's return.

I can't explain it.
And I don't need to.

Because peace didn't come
for approval—
it came for me.

And it stayed.

Selah Reflection

Peace isn't the absence of problems. It's the presence of God in the midst of them. When His peace comes, it doesn't ask permission—it takes its place.

Spiritual Challenge

Pray: "God, I receive peace I don't have to earn or explain." Then let stillness settle in.

Breath Prayer:
Inhale: "The silence has ended."
Exhale: "My soul still sings."

You made it through.
Let your praise be shaped by everything you survived.

This Praise Has Scars

"He brought me up... out of a horrible pit... and set my feet upon a rock... He has put a new song in my mouth." — Psalm 40:2-3 (NKJV)

This praise limps.
It doesn't run,
doesn't soar—
but it stands.

It has scars—
stories that sing louder
than the melody itself.

This praise knows pits.
Knows silence.
Knows wrestling.

And that's what makes it
holy.

It didn't come cheap.
Didn't come quick.
It came through fire,
and now it carries a fragrance
only the broken recognize.
This is not the song
of the unscarred.
This is the anthem
of the rescued.

Selah Reflection

Your scars don't disqualify your worship—they deepen it. Praise born from pain is a sound that shakes heaven in a different way.

Spiritual Challenge

Look at one scar—physical or emotional—and say: "You turned even this into a song."

Breath Prayer:
Inhale: "The silence has ended."
Exhale: "My soul still sings."

You made it through.
Let your praise be shaped by everything you survived.

The Sound of Joy Returning

"You turned my mourning into dancing... and clothed me with gladness."
— *Psalm 30:11 (ESV)*

It started small—
a hum,
a laugh I didn't force,
a moment of wonder
I didn't chase.

Joy came back
like a friend
who didn't knock,
just opened the door
and said,
"I never left for good."

I didn't trust it at first.
Thought maybe it was premature.

But it stayed.
And I wept
not because I was sad—
but because joy felt
like home again.
And its sound
wasn't loud—
it was steady.
It was mine.

Selah Reflection
Joy returns not with fireworks, but often with a whisper. Don't question it when it comes. Just welcome it. Let it live in you again.

Spiritual Challenge
Name one small moment today that brought joy. Say, "You are welcome here." Let joy know it has permission to stay.

Breath Prayer:
Inhale: "The silence has ended."
Exhale: "My soul still sings."

You made it through.
Let your praise be shaped by everything you survived.

Nothing Missing But the Weight
"That you may be perfect and complete, lacking nothing."
—James 1:4 (NKJV)

I didn't get back everything I lost.
Some things stayed buried,
some prayers went unanswered—
at least in the way I asked.

But I don't feel empty.
I feel full.
Whole,
even if not unchanged.

Grace didn't replace every piece.
It just removed the weight
that made me forget
I was still held.

I lack nothing now.
Not because I have it all,
but because the ache
doesn't rule me anymore.

The pain left.
The purpose stayed.
And peace
took its place.

Selah Reflection
Wholeness doesn't mean everything was restored. Sometimes it means the weight is gone, and the joy has room to rise again. You're not lacking—you're lighter.

Spiritual Challenge
Say: "I don't have everything, but I'm not missing anything." Let that become your posture of peace today.

Breath Prayer:
Inhale: "The silence has ended."
Exhale: "My soul still sings."

You made it through.
Let your praise be shaped by everything you survived.

The Answer Was Already in Me

"If the Spirit of Him who raised Jesus from the dead dwells in you... He will also give life to your mortal bodies..." — Romans 8:11 (ESV)

I searched outside
for something
God had already planted
within.
I waited for a sign,
a word,
a change in the weather.
But the wind of the Spirit
was already blowing
inside my ribcage.

I wasn't without answers—
I just hadn't learned
to listen to the presence
within me.

Resurrection power
was never far off.
It was in me—
breathing,
stirring,
waiting to be trusted.
Now I know.
Now I listen differently.
Now I move
with what's already mine.

Selah Reflection

You don't have to beg for what God already placed inside you. The Spirit within you is power, wisdom, and peace. You carry more than you think.

Spiritual Challenge

Whisper this prayer: "Spirit of God, I trust what You've placed in me." Let that change how you move today.

Breath Prayer:
Inhale: "The silence has ended."
Exhale: "My soul still sings."

You made it through.
Let your praise be shaped by everything you survived.

I Don't Need the Whole Picture to Praise
"Though the fig tree does not bud... yet I will rejoice in the Lord..."
— Habakkuk 3:17–18 (NIV)

The story's not finished.
The page is mid-turn.
The ending's unclear—
but my praise
is not on pause.

Because I've learned
that worship
doesn't wait
for clarity.

It waits for trust.

And trust
has taught me
to raise my hands
with eyes still blurry,
to sing
when the miracle's still forming.
I don't need
the whole picture
to know the Painter.
So I praise—
not because I see it all,
but because I know
the One who does.

Selah Reflection
Real worship happens before you understand. Trust is the frame around your unfinished story. Praise Him mid-sentence.

Spiritual Challenge
Write or speak one sentence of praise today that begins with: "Even though I don't know..."

Breath Prayer:
Inhale: "The silence has ended."
Exhale: "My soul still sings."

You made it through.
Let your praise be shaped by everything you survived.

The Quiet Has a New Meaning Now
"I have calmed and quieted my soul... like a weaned child with its mother..."
— *Psalm 131:2 (NIV)*

The silence used to scare me.
It felt like distance,
like rejection in disguise.

But now—
the quiet comforts me.

Because now I know
what it means:
You're near,
and I don't have to perform.

I've learned
how to sit with You
without filling the space.

Just presence.
Just breath.
Just trust.

The silence hasn't changed—
I have.

And now,
it feels like rest.

Selah Reflection
When you know God's heart, silence stops feeling like punishment and starts feeling like peace. Let the quiet draw you into deeper trust.
Spiritual Challenge
Spend one quiet moment today without speaking. Just sit with God. Let your calm soul be your prayer.

Breath Prayer:
Inhale: "The silence has ended."
Exhale: "My soul still sings."

You made it through.
Let your praise be shaped by everything you survived.

I Still Sing (And Always Will)
"I will praise the Lord all my life; I will sing praise to my God as long as I live." — Psalm 146:2 (NIV)

The storm didn't steal my song.
It bent it.
Stretched it.
Changed its tone—
but didn't silence it.
I still sing.
Not because everything's perfect,
but because grace
taught me how to find melody
in the ache.
My voice remembers
the valleys.
My praise wears the sound
of someone
who made it through.
And now—
whether loud or low,
public or whispered—
I will sing.
Not just today,
but always.

Because the silence ended,
but the song?
It's just beginning.

Selah Reflection
You've been through the silence and the storm, and still—you sing. That's your testimony. Your praise now carries legacy.
Spiritual Challenge
Speak this over yourself: "I still sing. And I always will."
Let that be your anthem today.

Go and Sing Again

Go now—
not as the same soul who walked in with questions,
but as one who has touched the silence
and lived to write about it.

You have wept in the quiet.
You have stood when your knees gave way.
You have dared to whisper when the world told you to wail.
And still—
you sang.

So take this song with you.
Take it to the broken places.
To the weary and the watching.
To the child in you who still wonders if
God remembers their name.
Take it to your neighbor.

To your church.
To the places justice has yet to reach.

And when you sing—
don't sing soft.

Sing like your freedom depends on it.
Sing like healing is still holy work.
Sing like the Gospel is not only preached,
but lived in bread, in balm,
in **every shoulder you make room for beneath your own
cross.**

Let your life be a long note of mercy.
Let your hands be instruments of grace.
Let your laughter—yes, your laughter—
be the echo of resurrection in a land that still mourns.
Storms will come again.

You will taste rain and dust again.
You will pray through clenched fists again.

But remember this:

There is rest between the roaring.
There is music beneath the rubble.
There is God—even there.

So go.
Sing your new song.
Bless boldly.
Love with holy audacity.
And when the next storm rises—
meet it with a melody
you learned in this stillness.

Selah,
and Amen.

Dave Joseph Jr. is a poet, pastor, and spiritual caregiver who believes deeply in the sacredness of silence, the resilience of the soul, and the power of God to speak between storms. Through writing, counseling, and community leadership, he invites others to wrestle honestly with life, love, and faith— and to find grace in the quiet places.

If this book spoke to your soul, consider sharing a copy with someone who's still in the storm.
You can also subscribe for more reflections at:

Connect at: www.poetpastor.substack.com

Selah Together: *A Journey Shared*

Opening Reflection: Why We Pause Together

Storms are loud. Healing is often quiet.

We live in a world that praises the noise of achievement but struggles to honor the hush of healing. This book, and this group journey, is an invitation into something slower, deeper, and more honest.

When we gather with others who are also walking through or remembering storms, we create something sacred—a space where courage meets compassion, where silence becomes a sanctuary, and where vulnerability is not weakness but worship.

This isn't about fixing each other. It's about being with one another.

So come. Bring your raw pages. Bring your laughter and your ache. Let us selah—pause and reflect—together.

Group Guidelines: Creating a Safe Selah Space

To make this space sacred, we agree to:

- **Speak from the "I"** – Share your story, not someone else's.
- **Respect the silence** – Every pause is part of the prayer.
- **No fixing, no preaching** – Presence is more healing than advice.
- **Hold each other's stories in confidence** – What's shared here stays here.
- **Honor all emotions** – Tears, laughter, and silence all belong.

Selah Together: A Journey Shared

Week 1 – Wounds & Whispers

Theme: *Honesty with God and self in seasons of pain*

This section explores what it means to be held in the middle of heartache, to speak softly into the silence, and to find that God is still whispering when everything else feels like it's fallen apart.

Suggested Reading

Read 2–3 poems from Section 1 aloud in the group. Recommended starting poems:
- *Lament with No Return Address*
- *I Still Belong*
- *God Doesn't Flinch*

Encourage group members to choose a line that stayed with them.

Reflection Questions
(Choose 2–3 for discussion)

1. Which poem in this section felt closest to your own story right now—and why?
2. Have you ever experienced a time when God's silence felt overwhelming? What did you learn in that space?
3. What does the word Selah mean to you after reading these poems?
4. How do you tend to respond in seasons of pain—withdraw, reach out, overfunction, collapse?
5. What would it look like to trust God in a whisper, not just in a shout?

Selah Together: *A Journey Shared*

You made it through.
Let your praise be shaped by everything you survived.

Selah Together: A Journey Shared

Creative Group Activities (Optional)

1. Selah Journaling
Invite members to write for 5–10 minutes in response to this prompt:
> "God, here is the storm I'm still holding..."

Those who feel comfortable can share what they've written.

2. Whispered Line Circle
Each person shares a single line or phrase from a poem in the section that spoke to them.
Go around the circle slowly. Let the room breathe between each line.
This creates a collective "poem" of healing voices.

3. Anointing With Words
Offer a word or short blessing to the person seated on your left (e.g., "You are not alone." "God still sees you."). Speak it gently and personally.

Closing Group Blessing (Read Aloud Together)

Blessed are the bruised who still show up.

Blessed are the whisperers, the watchers, the wounded,
who didn't wait to be whole before they shared their story.

May your pain be a doorway, not a prison.

May your silence carry songs no one else can sing.

May your soul find companions in the quiet.

And may you bless others—not with perfection,
but with presence.

Selah, and Amen.

Selah Together: A Journey Shared

Week 2 – Still Waters & Slow Miracles

Theme: *Learning to trust God in the waiting, even when movement feels miles away*

Waiting is rarely quiet on the inside. It churns with questions, doubts, and delays that test our trust. But Scripture is full of holy pauses, and this week invites us to honor that sacred stillness—not as a punishment, but as preparation.

Suggested Reading

Read 2–3 poems from Section 2 aloud in the group. Recommended starting poems:

- *Still Doesn't Mean Stuck*
- *When the Promise Feels Like a Lie*
- *If the Wind Never Comes*

Encourage group members to choose a line that stayed with them.

Reflection Questions

1. Which poem best described a season where you felt stuck or unheard by God?
2. What emotions does waiting stir in you—fear, frustration, fatigue, or something else?
3. When have you seen God do something after you gave up hope?
4. What's the difference between being "still" and being "stuck"?
5. How does today's culture challenge or contradict the spiritual gift of waiting?

Selah Together: *A Journey Shared*

You made it through.
Let your praise be shaped by everything you survived.

Selah Together: A Journey Shared

Creative Group Activities (Optional)

1. Waiting Wall
Invite each person to write a word or phrase on a Post-it note or card that represents what they're waiting on (healing, direction, peace, etc.). Place them together on a wall, board, or altar space. Pray over them as a group.

2. Silent 3-Minute Reflection
Set a timer. No music, no talking. Just silence. Ask group members to notice what they feel, think, or hear in their soul. Afterward, share what arose. Waiting always brings something up.

3. Letter from the Future
Invite each person to write a 2-minute letter from their future self, looking back on the season they're in now—speaking encouragement and faith to the "them" that's still waiting.

Closing Group Blessing (Read Aloud Together)

May you trust what hasn't moved
just as much as what has.

May you know that delay
is not denial,
and stillness
is not failure.

May the God who waited
for Lazarus, for Moses,
for you—
show you that waiting is woven with wisdom.

May you carry the promise,
even when it feels like a lie.

And when your faith falters,
may your doubt become a doorway
into deeper love.

Selah, and Amen.

Selah Together: A Journey Shared

Week 3 – Bittersweet Waters

Theme: *The long journey of healing—when faith returns slowly, and forgiveness still stings*

Healing is holy work, but it is not always clean or quick. Bitterness and sweetness often flow together in the same soul. This week is an invitation to drink deeply from both—without rushing, numbing, or pretending the wounds never existed.

Suggested Reading

Choose 2–3 poems to read aloud and reflect upon:
- *I Forgave, but I Still Remember*
- *I Want to Believe Again*
- *It Was Sweet All Along*

Reflection Questions

1. Which line or poem helped you name something you've buried?
2. What does forgiveness feel like to you—freedom, fear, unfinished?
3. Have you ever experienced the kind of redemption Joseph speaks of in Genesis 50:20?
4. What's harder for you—believing again, or forgiving again? Why?
5. Where do you feel God is turning bitter water into something sweet in your story?

Selah Together: *A Journey Shared*

You made it through.
Let your praise be shaped by everything you survived.

Selah Together: A Journey Shared

Creative Group Activities (Optional)

1. Memory Stone Activity
Give each person a small smooth stone. On one side, invite them to write (or imagine writing) something they remember that still hurts. On the other side, a word of what they're choosing to carry forward (e.g., "hope," "wisdom," "mercy"). Pray silently, then invite a few to share.
2. Forgiveness Letter (Unsent)
Have each person begin a short letter to someone they're learning to forgive. This letter is not for sending—it's for releasing. Encourage honesty. "I forgive you, but I still feel…" is welcome here.
3. Bitter to Sweet Tasting (if in-person)
Use a simple object lesson: pass out lemon slices and honey. Taste the lemon first—bitterness, sting, sharpness. Then taste the honey. Reflect silently or aloud on where each flavor shows up in their healing journey.

Closing Group Blessing (Read Aloud Together)

May the waters that once made you bitter
become the well from which others drink.

May your memories teach you,
but never chain you.

May you forgive without forgetting—
not because you must,
but because you're becoming free.

And when believing again feels hard,
may you hear God's voice say:
                Do not fear. Just believe."

May sweetness surprise you in unexpected places.

May healing come slowly, but surely.

May your scars tell stories of survival, not shame.

Selah, and Amen.

Selah Together: *A Journey Shared*

Week 4 – Stillness Between Struggles

Theme: *Holding on in the middle of the night when the breakthrough hasn't come yet*

There are nights when morning feels like a myth. In the darkness, faith doesn't always roar—it sometimes sighs, weeps, or waits in stillness. This week helps us honor those "midnight moments" and find strength in the promise that even silence has a sunrise.

Suggested Reading

Read 2–3 poems aloud and reflect together:
- *Midnight Feels Like Forever*
- *There's a Hallelujah in the Hurt*
- *This Night Will Not Last Forever*

Reflection Questions

1. What poem (or line) resonated with your midnight moment?
2. Have you ever struggled to believe that joy will return? What helped or hindered that belief?
3. What does it mean to you to "bless the Lord at all times"?
4. How do you handle long seasons of waiting between the breakdown and breakthrough?
5. What does faithfulness look like on a night when nothing changes?

Selah Together: *A Journey Shared*

You made it through.
Let your praise be shaped by everything you survived.

Selah Together: *A Journey Shared*

Creative Group Activities (Optional)

1. Candlelight Reflection
Dim the lights and light a candle in the center. Have each person name (aloud or silently) a night they've survived—or are still surviving. Reflect in silence together, then speak the promise: **"This night will not last forever."**

2. Mercy List
Invite group members to write a list of "new mercies" they've seen recently (big or small). Share 1–2 with the group as an act of remembering.

3. Midnight Testimony Circle
Each person shares a "midnight story" from their life—what it felt like, how they endured, and what they're still learning. Close with the group blessing below.

Closing Group Blessing (Read Aloud Together)

May your midnight become a meeting place.

May the ache in your chest
become the altar where mercy kneels beside you.

May you bless the Lord not because it's easy,
but because it's honest.

May you believe again—
that mornings still come,
that tears still dry,
that hope is still holy.

And when you have nothing left but breath,
may your breath be a hallelujah.

Selah, and Amen.

Selah Together: *A Journey Shared*

Week 5 – Broken Hallelujahs

Theme: *Letting grace meet the places shame tried to bury*

Grace doesn't come for the polished. It meets us in the rubble, the regret, and the places where we don't feel worthy. This week invites you to remember that God not only forgives—He forgets. Not because He's careless, but because He's kind.

Suggested Reading

Read 2–3 of the following poems together:
- *Forgiven Doesn't Mean Forgotten*
- *The Shame Grace Refused to Carry*
- *The Grace I Can't Repay*

Encourage group members to underline a phrase that spoke directly to their soul.

Reflection Questions

1. Which poem felt most personal—and why?
2. How do you wrestle with the difference between being forgiven and still remembering your own failures?
3. What has shame tried to make you believe about yourself that grace is trying to undo?
4. Can you recall a time when grace came before you felt ready—or worthy?
5. What would it look like to live as someone truly free from condemnation?

Selah Together: *A Journey Shared*

You made it through.
Let your praise be shaped by everything you survived.

Selah Together: *A Journey Shared*

Creative Group Activities (Optional)

1. Torn Pages & Grace Notes
Give each person a sheet of paper and have them write down a moment of shame or regret. Fold it. Tear it. Crumple it. Then pass out a new card to write a "grace note"—a word or phrase God might say in response (e.g., "Loved," "Still Mine," "Clean"). Share only the second card aloud if desired.

2. Broken Hallelujah Playlist
Play a few quiet songs that speak of grace (e.g., "You Say" by Lauren Daigle, "Broken Vessels" by Hillsong, "No Longer Slaves"). Let each person reflect silently or write down what their "broken hallelujah" sounds like.

3. Hands of Grace
Invite group members to look at their own hands. Have them imagine one thing those hands did that they regret—and then one thing God might now do through them. End by placing hands gently over hearts and praying silently.

Closing Group Blessing (Read Aloud Together)

May your shame lose its grip,
and may grace take its place.

May you remember that you are not the sum of what you did—
but the song of the One who redeemed it.

May you be free from the prison of perfection,
and embrace the kind of mercy
that kneels beside your mess and says:
"You're still Mine."

May you sing hallelujahs,
even when your voice shakes,
because grace is the echo in your silence.

You are forgiven.

You are loved.

You are not forgotten.

Selah, and Amen.

Selah Together: *A Journey Shared*

Week 6 – Becoming in the Dark

Theme: *Letting God shape you quietly—through shadows, stillness, and unseen strength*

Some of God's best work is done in the dark—buried seeds, quiet caves, wilderness places. Growth isn't always loud. Transformation doesn't always trend. This week reminds us that God sees every detail, and even the tremble of your soul has meaning.

Suggested Reading

Read 2–3 poems aloud and invite slow reflection:
- *I Found God in the Details*
- *The Ground Still Trembles, But I Don't*
- *The Whisper After the Storm*

Encourage group members to circle a line that made them pause or feel seen.

Reflection Questions

1. Which poem helped you feel seen by God in your unseen places?
2. What parts of your life feel like they're still "in the dark"? How is God moving there?
3. What have you discovered about yourself (or God) after the storm passed?
4. Can you share a time when God's whisper spoke louder than a shout?
5. How do you define strength now compared to earlier in your journey?

Selah Together: *A Journey Shared*

You made it through.
Let your praise be shaped by everything you survived.

Selah Together: A Journey Shared

Creative Group Activities (Optional)

1. The Hidden Work
Give everyone a seed (or simply show a picture). Reflect on what has to happen in the dark before it can bloom. Invite each person to name one part of their life that's being shaped silently. Pray over one another for growth below the surface.

2. Detail Cards
Have each person write 3 small "details" about themselves they think go unnoticed (e.g., "I hide when I'm anxious," "I love quiet mornings," "I still miss my childhood pastor"). Then invite God into those details—ask the group to write one word God would say about each one.

3. Whisper Walk
Take a silent walk indoors or outdoors. Let each person listen for a word or phrase that comes to their spirit—not out loud, but inwardly. After 3–5 minutes, return and share the whisper if they feel led.

Closing Group Blessing (Read Aloud Together)

May you find the God who counts hairs,
names shadows,
and speaks in silence.

May the ground quake—
but may you not.

May you trust the whisper
more than the whirlwind,
the stillness
more than the storm.

In the dark, may you bloom.

In the unknown, may you become.

God has not forgotten the quiet work He's doing in you.

The silence is not the end.

It's the shaping.

Selah, and Amen.

Selah Together: *A Journey Shared*

Week 7 – The Song That Remains

Theme: *Living with peace, joy, and praise after the storm*

Not every storm ends with noise. Sometimes it ends with stillness, resolve, and a quiet, unwavering praise. This week reminds us that the song of faith doesn't end when the trouble does—it deepens. This is not the conclusion of your journey, but the beginning of your testimony.

Suggested Reading

Read 2–3 poems aloud and reflect together:
- Nothing Missing But the Weight
- The Quiet Has a New Meaning Now
- I Still Sing (And Always Will)

Encourage group members to take a deep breath before and after each poem. Let the silence be part of the reflection.

Reflection Questions

1. Which poem captured how you feel now, after walking through previous weeks?
2. What has changed in your spirit over the course of these discussions?
3. What new meaning does quiet have in your life now?
4. What is your soul's "song" now—what truth keeps singing in you?
5. How can your story become someone else's healing?

Selah Together: *A Journey Shared*

You made it through.
Let your praise be shaped by everything you survived.

Selah Together: A Journey Shared

Creative Group Activities (Optional)

1. Your Soul's Chorus
Each person writes a one-sentence "song" or declaration from their journey (e.g., "I'm still standing," "Peace holds me now," "The storm didn't win"). Read them aloud like a group chant. Repeat together.
2. Testimony Threads
On a long sheet of butcher paper or in a shared document, invite group members to write one moment or breakthrough from the journey that surprised them. It can be small. Together, it creates a tapestry of faith.
3. Peace Exchange
Each person writes a short blessing for the person seated next to them—something simple like "May joy surprise you tomorrow," or "You are safe, seen, and whole." Exchange and read quietly.

Closing Group Blessing (Read Aloud Together)

May you walk into tomorrow
lighter,
softer,
stronger.

May the quiet now feel like home,
not fear.

May the storm lose its sting,
but leave behind a song.

May you know, with holy assurance,
that nothing is missing
but the weight.

That you are still here,
still whole,
still His.

And may your life sing—
not for applause,
but for the One who danced with you in the dark.

Selah, and Amen.

Selah Together: A Journey Shared
Final Group Reflection Prompts

Choose one or more to discuss as a group:

Looking Back: What part of this journey surprised you the most?
Healing in Community: How has this group helped you grow or let go?
Lingering Truth: What truth from these poems do you carry with you now?
Continued Selah: Where do you need to pause next—in life, in faith, or in your relationships?
Next Step: What storm or story are you now ready to speak into someone else's life?

Personal Reflection

Today I am grateful for…

One storm I survived…

One line or poem I will return to…

My song sounds like…

My prayer moving forward…

Group Leader's Blessing
(Optional to Read Aloud or Personalize)

May the One who led you through
now lead you forward.
May you never forget that healing is not a race,
but a rhythm.
May these poems echo in your prayers,
and may your story become someone else's survival song.
Don't stop singing.
Don't stop resting.
And don't forget—
there are others still in the storm
who need to hear the song that remains in you.

Selah, and Amen.
You made it through.
Let your praise be shaped by everything you survived.

www.ingramcontent.com/pod-product-compliance
Lightning Source LLC
Chambersburg PA
CBHW030113240426
43673CB00002B/65